Guardian of Lost Souls

Lessons in Death

www.guardianoflostsouls.com

Pamela Theresa Loertscher, M. Msc.

Copyright © 2008 by Pamela Theresa Loertscher

Published by: Pamela Theresa Loertscher
www.guardinoflostsouls.com
pamela@guardianoflostsouls.com

ISBN: 1440491429

Contents

PART 1 - DISCOVERY OF THE SOUL

PART 2 – THE SPARK OF THE DIVINE

PART 3 – THE LOST SOULS

APPENDIX

Preface

This book is intended to teach about the spaces in-between, and was written especially for many who are questioning about similar types of experiences...

If you are one who feels, hears, and sees the world of spirit, as you read the pages that follow, you may experience and feel a sense of finally belonging to this world in which we live.

The best analogy that I have found came to me one morning from my husband David. He told me that this is a book that is much like a pregnant woman explaining to another pregnant woman the experiences of carrying a child in the womb. However, if you are a man it would be impossible for me to fully explain the experience because you have not experienced carrying and giving birth to a child.

I write this book knowing full well that there is no way for me to prove that these things have happened to me, besides the fact that I *know* that they have. Through my journeys I have felt as most people might think—that some of my experiences must be a delusion. I have thought this of myself many times in my life. I do not judge those out there who feel this way about me, however I am human and it does sting a bit especially when it comes from friends and family members. Also, it is not my intent to convince the skeptic whose sole purpose may be in trying to prove me wrong because as I say all of the time; "*I am not a dog and pony show*".

It is my hope that the pages within this book will offer a validation to those who experience seeing earthbounds, spirits and angels—I know all to well that there is much to see and experience in the spaces in-between, and it can get confusing sometimes. I do know however that these experiences are based in foundation from our heart center—if we so choose to believe. For me it is a knowing coupled with the energies that I feel, hear and see.

I do believe that we all posses the gifts and ability to feel, hear and see, it is simply a matter of choice. Many are clueless to the gifts that lie within, and are ignorant to the mass amounts of treasure within the soul. These simple treasures offer the answers to *ALL* questions.

This has been a difficult journey for me…to reveal my personal truths. The world in which we live can be skeptical and because of this, my default reaction has been to hide. I am now grateful that I did find the courage to "*come out of the spiritual closet*", thank you ever so much for opening your heart and allowing me to share my story with you.

A Special Note:

The names that I have given to the lost souls in this book are not as important as the information that they gave me about their lifetime here on this earth, and also the work they continue to do-- even now. Names seem to be more difficult, because our names change as do our lifetimes, so I could be connected to the energy of a soul and feel that his name was Joe, but in fact his name might have been Jack in this life, but Joseph in a previous life. Then there is the factor that we have names that we chose to go by on the otherside, so I could actually be picking up on their true name...who knows? In other words, I do not put too much importance on their names because I am aware of the intricacies of the energies. Nevertheless, if you find a story about one of the lost souls and you feel that it is about your loved one, except the fact that the name was wrong, but everything else was spot on, then chances are the person of whom I am speaking of is indeed your loved one...trust me, you will know. Regardless of the situation, I hope these stories can offer healing and hope for all who read them.

Love always,

Pamela

Introduction

Who is the Guardian of Lost Souls?

Who is the Guardian? The short answer is that we are <u>all</u> the guardian of lost souls. Throughout my experiences of helping the lost souls to the other side, I kept hearing the phrase from spirit, "*guardian*". I always assumed that the message coming to me was bits and pieces of information regarding my guardian angel. Through time I learned that part of my interpretation of the message was indeed correct, although I had no idea of the scope and magnitude of the word that was delivered to me through spirit. In fact, when I eventually heard, or rather allowed myself to hear the message in full, I did not embrace the idea that I was a guardian of lost souls. For me that meant that I had a working title, and there was a part of me that felt that if I accepted it, there would never be an end to helping earthbounds to the other side. I was definitely not ready to accept that crazy idea. In fact, I was hoping that what had happened in my life was a little blip on the screen of my existence and that hopefully it would go away as soon as I had mastered it and learned how to control it. I was in deep research mode to find a way to make everything stop, and there was a weird notion in my mind that each time would be the last. I no longer wanted to deal with earthbound energies. I wanted to be free of the thought of death and blood and pain. When I heard the message in full it came to me as the wind blows through a tree… "*You are a guardian of lost souls*", the words echoed in my head. It did not occur to me at the time that spirit was trying to answer the question that I had asked over and over again since I had had my first visit with Piper. *"Why is this happing to me and my kids?"* I must have asked that question a million times over of Mother-Father God when the earthbounds kept coming into our home and personal space.

Through time and allowing the messages from spirit to flow through my being I learned that there are many different types of guardians. There are those in the skin who work as earth angels and their life's work is to help those in the skin who are lost, lonely, and in need of help. The most interesting fact about this type of guardian is that they don't even know that they are working as a guardian- as an extension of God's light and love to help those in need. They simply have a profoundly deep and soulful purpose which naturally flows through their being—a natural wanting to help others. It is their life mission and they simply can not *not* help others. This is a great example of a soul's mission and purpose on earth manifesting in natural order. Oftentimes we do things and we are drawn to certain circumstances that naturally guide us to our divine life purpose.

There are also many souls who are now in spirit who help us from the otherside. They walk the earth and create miracles from the spaces in-between to help us in any way we will allow them to do so. They have much power to help move things around so that our lives can flow in the direction of our chosen purpose.

A most beautiful discovery was when we experienced former lost souls who came and helped us with other lost souls…the work they do now is in working with people like us in helping to guide the lost souls to the light. They are guardians of lost souls.

Animal spirit guides are the beautiful transmitter of healing energies, much in the same way our physical animals create a beautiful loving and powerful healing energy. They are also guardians and help us in so many ways often unknown.

The Masters such as Jesus, Mother Mary, and Yogananda do much work in the spaces in-between to help the lost souls find their way back home to heaven. They too walk between the two worlds. The Masters work much with the angelic realms in the organizational process to help bring order to seeming chaos. They love to help bring in family members who are in spirit to help guide the lost soul back home.

Mother-Father God gifted to us the most magnificent guardians and protectors—the angelic realms! The angels are the ultimate when it comes to the guardian of lost souls. My work in helping lost souls always begins with angels and ends with angels... they are ever present working the spaces in-between. The angelic realms are the hand of Mother-Father God to bring about order to chaos, light to darkness, and when necessary they help to transform the energies into love. Without this work gifted to us from our Heavenly Mother and Father, it would be impossible for us to physically live on this earth. Archangel Michael orchestrates and works with people like me in helping lost souls find their way back home. He really is the go to angel in the world of earthbound spirits. *He is, in my heart, **The Guardian of Lost Souls.***

This book is dedicated to the guardians of the lost souls...to those who work effortlessly with love, joy and great purpose to help all whom are in need of love and comfort. Together, the angels, masters, and guides help all who are lost, it matters not if it be "in the skin" or "in spirit"...they are ever present creating beautiful miracles, guiding all to the light of God's love. Many a time the words are echoed through the energies from the lost souls to the guardians:
"Thank you dear one for helping me-
I once was lost but now I'm found."
My eternal love is freely coursing through my being to Mother – Father God and Their beautiful heavenly helpers of love and light. Love always, Pamela
~ Om, Peace, Amen ~

Part 1

Discovery of the Soul

Chapter 1

The Wind of Change to the Road Less Traveled

It was getting late in the afternoon, and many of the readers of the little Cassadaga, Florida Spiritualist Camp had called it a day. My friend and I had traveled a two hour drive to visit the historic town to get a reading from a spiritual medium. I was scared half out of my wits because I had never done a thing like this before—this was my first time. After spending several hours exploring the shops in the tiny spiritual town, my friend and I settled on getting a reading from one of the mediums that was listed on a board in the camp bookstore. I was browsing around the store as my friend went to the whiteboard and started calling out the names to me, she told me that I should go with my feelings of who should give me the reading. When she read the name Joan Piper, I quickly came back into the moment from my daydream state. The name hit the right note for me…Piper, as I knew I would call her, for me that was her name.

"Piper, Piper"…I whispered the name over and over again in my head…the name felt so familiar. It was as if a bell

went off in my head, and I knew instantly that she was the one, she was the person who would give me the reading. I was actually going to do this thing!

Because I was in unchartered waters and did not know what to expect, I asked my friend if she would go first and get a feel for Piper. I decided that if my friend did not like Piper I would cancel my reading. I talked my friend into agreeing to attend my session, although she told me that the medium may not be willing to do so. She told me that most readers won't agree to do personal readings with others in the room and that quite often there is personal information that really should not be shared with others, and that it was a privacy issue. My friend went up the stairs to Pipers home and went inside. I waited for what seemed like hours. I sat in the meditation garden. I moved around and paced like a caged animal. I knew that something important in my life was about to happen, I just did not know what it was. I was chain smoking and biting my cheeks in anticipation of my reading.

Although I was excited, I was nervous as well. I pondered what she might reveal to me. Was I going to die soon? Was my life headed into another disaster? Would she be a fraud? What did she look like? My hands and face were sweating and the Florida July heat did not help me either. I finally sat down on a cement bench facing the meditation pond, and out of nowhere my grandpa whispered into my ear a stern warning. He told me that under no uncertain terms should I interrupt during the reading and that I needed to keep my mouth shut and let the woman talk. He knew me well because when I get nervous I have a tendency to babble. I start talking and I can't seem to shut my mouth. He told me over and over to keep my lips zipped shut. He told me to simply listen to what Piper was about to tell me. Finally, I agreed. I think I agreed with him so he would stop hounding me. He was insistent that I follow his instructions to keep my mouth from moving. After what seemed to be forever, my friend immerged from Pipers home with a smile on her face. She told me that I must go in alone as Piper could not do a reading with both of us—she said that it would interfere with the energy of the reading, so I agreed.

As I walked up the stairs to Pipers home an energy of calm engulfed my body, and I could feel the air pressure around my body change to a soothing calm. The wind chimes that were hung from the porch were dancing in the wind, creating beautiful sounds of random music. It was an inviting home and the porch had little crystals, and pots of flowers placed about here and there. Piper greeted me at the door with a beaming smile and a hug. She looked normal enough to me, and I felt her loving energy immediately. I felt safe with her. I looked at her and was overcome with a feeling of familiarity— it was as if we had met before, although I knew that we had not. I followed her into the sitting room, and took a look around the room at the beautiful angels and crystals placed about the room. Her surroundings were inviting and homey. She had a tape playing ever so softly in the background of beautiful nature sounds…my favorite sounds. The music calmed me and as I sat down at the table, a smile crossed my lips. The table was covered in a beautiful lace tablecloth, (*I love pretty things like lace and flowers*). I handed her the tape that I purchased at the camp bookstore, so that my session could be recorded. I observed quietly as she wrote the date of July 1, 2006 side A. Immediately it flew through my mind: *"Oh, she's a south paw!"* I thought of my oldest son Jesse who was a lefty and thought maybe Piper and I could be kindred spirits. Instinctually, I think my mind was trying to find a way to connect with her, as I was still a bit afraid. The thought of my son was calming and familiar. I relaxed my body and settled into the chair. She took my hands and said a little prayer. After the prayer she turned on the tape recorder to record my session—the reading had officially started.

I remember thinking to myself that if she were a fraud I would certainly know. I knew that grandpa was there with me, and if she didn't notice him, that would be a dead give away…no pun intended. I know that to some it would seem to be the obvious, a no brainer. Because most people at my age have a dead grandpa. However, for me it would be validation. She started the reading, as she talked my mind wandered a bit. I was trying so hard to concentrate on what she was telling me, but because my mind chatter was in the way, half of what she said went in one ear and out the other. She spoke to me about my children and how I homeschooled them. She talked to me about my daughter, and how she had the ability to see the angels and communicate with spirit. She grabbed my attention when she spoke the word hospice to me. She told me that I had hospice written all over me and that there was a real magnet there. My head started to swirl as I thought she was about to tell me that I had a terminal illness and that I would be spending the rest of my days in a hospice. Almost immediately, my mind started to grasp for an excuse to abruptly leave the reading. My initial fears of a reading had been realized. My mind was telling me that she was about to give me a death sentence, and I had no intention of letting anyone give me that spooky news! I think she must have noticed the pasty shade of my face, nevertheless, she continued as if nothing unusual had been said. Piper started by telling me that there is part of me for the aptitude for helping people out. She said that spirit was showing her things that I was capable of doing, and that it did not feel like now, but that spirit never gives a time table and that it felt like later on. She then said that she was going to tell me why and that she did not want it to scare me or frighten me or any of the above.

She was proceeding gently— *"You know that part that you don't like about death? That part terrifies you. Well, sometimes there's a reason for those emotions. There are actually things that you see that scares you. Now, we are going to put a good simple twist on this, so you are going to feel very good about it."* She smiled at me and continued. *"It's actually a gift that you have, and I don't want to take it away from you."* She paused for a second, and then continued. *"If you were with a person, and I mean it in a very lovely way, and they were getting ready to pass, you could actually see who they were talking to. You would know where they were going to go...you would know where it is. Its there because spirit is showing me this...okay..."* I nodded my head and said *"I know"*, she giggled and said, *"I know you know. But I would want you to look at it the beautiful way, because there are so many people that die alone. They don't have anybody there. Or, for the people that don't have that gift that you really do have...it is truly there. By you just holding someone's hand, not only is it going to help them see the picture clearer, they are going to be able to have communication...its like they are going to say...ahhh...I see my husband, he's really coming...its Jack...he's here, and you are not only going to be able to feel him there, you are going to be able to describe him, so you are going to be able to help that person say yes, I really can go, I can really let this go. Also, issues... They are telling me about family issues. You know, when people pass, they do a lot of reviewing of their life."* She looked at me and nodded her head and said; *"but, you know that...you really do know that. Oh you have so seen this!"*

As Piper talked my mind went back to that moment in my car in a desolate parking lot just nine months before where I had given up on my life. As I sat in that car all alone in the parking lot, I reflected upon my life. It was a long trail of personal loss. The years of self neglect and abuse had resulted in a lack of personal respect. I had developed a deep dark hatred of myself. I was at a crossroads in my life. I sat staring in a stupor across the beautiful green grass that was in front of me, and I watched the maple branches sway as the wind swept through the trees. This was *The Wind of Change*, I had experienced this many times in my life, and I knew that it meant only one thing. Change.

The wind came with a vivid vision that always seemed to manifest itself. This particular wind was a picture of two paths. The paths were painted before my eyes in a colorful vision. One path that I saw was life, and the flow of more of the same. It was a deep and dark battle and I was worn out. I had no fight left in me—I was in the depths of despair. The other path was one of surrender. I interpreted this path as a sign that it was time to give up the fight for life. I wanted to quit living and I wanted to be totally annihilated. I had a deep desire to be zapped from the planet, and I craved total non-existence. As I sat in that stupor, I reflected upon my life with deep sorrow. I had been defeated. For me, all time stood still as I took a review of my life. I knew it and I felt it with every fiber of my being, I was a lost soul. The horrors that swirled around in my mind were of past events that I was eager to escape. What was wrong with me? If I had a penny for every time I thought that... I had no words to describe what I felt, and what was driving my fears. I had suffered for years with migraine headaches, and panic attacks in an attempt to push it all away. I spent years in a grip of fear, and I tried to keep control. Besides all of my problems of the past, I knew I was not "normal", and I constantly thought I was going crazy. This was just another thing I was trying escape and hide from. I would use code words such as I have a feeling this is a bad idea—never really explaining the fullness of the visions that freely flowed through my mind. These visions would always seem to come from out of nowhere. These visions were always attached to a strong feeling, and horrid smells. I would try to explain to my husband that I could see colors around people. I had a fear of talking about these things—I thought it would make me sound like a crazy and delusional person. My particular specialty was child molesters, creeps, I would call them. They always had a dark smoke wafting around their body. It would be accompanied with the smell of mildew, a musty, horrid smell. The worst part of this for me was the visions that I would see. I would see the act and watch in horror.

Try as I might, I could never escape the visions and they would come to me from out of nowhere. I was always left surprised by the visions because I did not know what was going on with me. I remember thinking what a horrible person I was to think thoughts like those about people, people that I did not even know. To the core of my being I knew the visions were real. Nevertheless, on some level I blamed myself for being judgmental over these people. Through the years I had discovered that when I was in close proximity to a person who has a strong emotion about an event in their life, I get a vision. This vision is a movie played out in my mind of the act, and their feelings that they are so entrenched with. Because I had never read any books about these strange things, I felt there was something seriously wrong with me. It never dawned on me that others might experience this as well.

I had instinctively learned through the years not to ignore the strong feelings and visions that I had. Every time I ignored them, it would backfire and I would wind up in a mess of some sort. I remember when I was young, my mom told me that my grandpa had the gift of discernment, and he also had hands that healed. Whatever that meant, I supposed that I had it too. However, I felt that what happened to me was some sort of curse.

Normal was never a word I would use to describe myself or the events that happened to me in my life. I think in an attempt to fight back, I just shut down and closed the whole world out. I used the combination of fight or flight. Fight—this was my angriness and bitter attitude. Flight—this was my isolated life, and I kept my distance from everyone. My life had boiled down to trips to the grocery store and shopping to meet the needs of my family. I could not name a single friend in over twelve years outside of my husband. Sitting alone in that car all of these thoughts swirled around in my head. The images of my life kept playing, it was a movie and I was trying to stop it. I tried in vain to push the visions of the past out of my head to no avail. I felt as though I was going mad. Just when I thought I could not take it anymore, it happened.

My mind started to slow down, the thoughts started fading away, and for the first time in my life I felt total silence—total peace. The silence seemed to come out of nowhere, everything around me slowed and the car filled with warm soothing air. The air pressure in the car started to change, it was comfortable and peaceful. I stared at the smoke from my cigarette, it stood almost at a complete standstill, forming interesting shapes and figures. I sat back in the seat and wondered if I was finally dying from a broken heart. I pondered of what I had heard about death, and how people finally make peace right before they make the transition. I was ready. I had come to terms with the end of my life, and I knew I was not alone in the car. I felt the warmth and love from him, grandpa had come to me, and I felt his eternal love, and a deep knowledge flowing into my being. Everything, everyone, all of the cars on the road moved at a snails pace, and then seemed to come to a complete stop.

My eyes drifted onto the maple tree in front of me. From atop the tree a leaf started to sway downwards toward the ground. It seemed to be the only thing moving around me. As that leaf slowly drifted downwards I saw the two paths before me again. I realized that the path of surrender was the path less traveled in my life, *had I ever even been down that road?* ...I thought about it, and I knew at once that the answer was a definite no. I had never even considered letting go of my grip of fear—I thought it was what kept me protected. I started to understand that the road less traveled was that of acceptance and forgiveness. I had a deep knowing that I needed to accept and forgive myself.

It is impossible to fully describe what happened in that car that day because it was more about a knowing, a knowing that can't be describe in any language. That day was the day my soul spoke to me, and for the first time in nearly 39 years, I listened. My soul whispered softly to my heart that I wasn't done yet, I had a purpose. This was the answer I had been seeking for years. It had been driving me nuts. I had a deep knowing that I was here on this planet for a reason, but I could never quite put a finger on it. As much as I tried to make my children my purpose,

I knew it was temporary as I did not own their souls, and I knew deep down that they would go on with their lives to complete their own life purpose. Anytime I would hear someone talk about life purpose, it would get to my core, and I was frustrated because I had a feeling I was nowhere near my purpose. I had been searching for a purpose to my life for years.

That day I saw the future through the road less traveled, and it instilled within my heart hope. Although, I did not have any idea of what my purpose entailed, I knew deep down that I finally had one. When I first parked that car, it was all I could do to hold my head up and yet now I was surging with a heavenly energy pulsating through my being that uplifted me. It was as if in a split second all of the weight of my life lifted from my shoulders and heart and left me feeling light, airy and loved. All of the sudden I knew what I had to do, I was elated and I was excited for the first time to live my life. I pondered in amazement at how swiftly one could change the course of ones life simply by acceptance of what had been and what would be. I pulled out of that empty parking lot a different person. As I backed the car away from the curb I looked at the tree and I knew on that day, the wind of change had come, one leaf fell and changed my life…altering my course forever onto the road less traveled…this was the road to love, surrender, and acceptance.

I listened in as Piper continued to speak. I knew what she was talking to me about because I had come to a place where I had wanted to end my life, so I nodded my head in agreement. She continued; *"They review their whole life, okay sometimes it takes them a week or two, but, usually the biggest part they do is in that last week before they die. They go through their whole life…they start from childhood until they are all the way up to where they are, and then that's when they are really that close to it. And they review it...but, for you to be there with them, and to see it, then they have that person communicating with them, and they know it, and they know it's not bad... it, it really is, it really is. It helps them on that journey...it makes it very peaceful for them...because, that is the moment where they have to make peace with themselves."*

Once again my mind went back in time to the parking lot. How many times in my life did I think to myself that I was going to die? How many times did I do a life review? I think I was pretty good at it by now. So, this was all starting to make sense to me. Maybe there is a rhyme to this reason of life after all. Through my experiences in my life I had developed an understanding...a gift of sorts. I had been to that moment where my life flashed before my eyes numerous times. I had even been to the reckoning of what was, and to the giving into the peace that was needed to leave this earth. I had been to the place of making peace with myself and my life. The reason that I did not die that day was starting to make sense to me. The whisperings in my heart from grandpa that I was not done yet, and that I had a greater purpose was revealing itself to me. I came back to the moment and continued to listen to Piper.

"You know God doesn't judge us, we judge ourselves. And you know that also. That's what makes you do life so well today. Because you know when you put your head on that pillow you want to have felt that you have done everything to the best of your ability, that you have loved everyone to the best of your ability. This is why you don't like to be angry. You don't, no not at all, because it really unbalances you."

Once again my mind altered to a state of the understanding that I had so recently come too—it used to infuriate me when people told me that everything in life happens for a reason. I personally felt that it was one big cruel joke, and that I was some sort of science experience gone bad. I used to feel that God was laughing at all of the foolish and stupid things I would do. I imagined him up there somewhere having a jolly old time at my expense saying things like: *"Look at her! She did it again!"*, as he would munch on his popcorn and slurp his heavenly soda in amusement. Yes, I was bitter, but especially at God. I was truly angry with whoever had created me and this horrible world. I would shake my fists towards the sky and dare Him to strike me dead, yet it never happened…each time it would leave me with a feeling that maybe He wasn't so bad after all, maybe this hell fire and damnation was a bunch of lies. Maybe He did truly love me. But then another thought would occur to me that maybe I was evil and not worth His time because I was lost to him anyhow. Nevertheless, each time that my life would go to hell, He was the always first I would blame. It wasn't always that way for me. When I was a little girl I used to love to think about God, Heaven, and Jesus. However, after a while, and a few hard knocks, I believed that I was on my own. I believed that no one cared about what happened to the little lonely girl. But now, in this time, my thinking had been altered by the drop of one leaf. I came to know in that moment that it was I who was passing judgment and creating the fear and damnation of my existence. I came to a profound inner wisdom that day that I was the one with the power to control my feelings. I entered a plane of existence where I felt the Divine and His eternal love for me. Words cannot describe the feeling of peace and the feeling of simply being. Engraved within my mind now, and forever more was an imprint of heavenly love and a knowing of unconditional love to all that was, all that is, and all that would be. Yes, I truly understood. I continued to listen, *"You do have the words and the strength to do this...this insight that you have. This is the spiritual gift that you have. You can do with it whatever you want. I am telling you that is what spirit is showing me—very simple, very easy."*

Piper paused for a moment then she started to speak again. Finally! The message that I had been waiting for... *"You have a grandfather in spirit?"* I remember thinking yep, this is right—this was the validation I was seeking. I nodded my head and whispered *"yes"*, she smiled and continued, *"This feels kind of special. It does. You know, you had some relatives that also saw and felt a whole lot. I really like him because he feels really loving, very loving, and it feels like you had a very good connection with each other, its like he was very happy that you were born. He was ecstatic that you were born. You were his little princess...that is what he is showing me. I am completely choked up with the kind of emotion that this man has. It's almost like people saw this other side to him that was always there, but he wasn't there to give it. But, with you he was able too. It's almost like he is thanking you for being born. It just feels very, very special here and he's telling me that he knows that you have these gifts. I am going to say that he saw a lot and felt a lot. But, just because life was the way it was, he wasn't able to do anything with it. He had to earn the money and take care of the family. He really felt that responsibility very heavy on his shoulders. He worked hard...hard, where I wish it could have been a lot easier on him."* Then she giggled and said, *"So, he is telling me about you okay. When you are ready, and you want to look into it, it's available to you. You have your free will and free choice...but, that's the part that gives you the hick-up with death*" Piper paused for a second and smiled at me, then she continued with the reading, "*Okay, when I see it, everybody has the doorway. You have many doorways that you can leave if you want to leave, or you could say, no not yet...I'm not ready this time. But, I truly feel like it's between you and God. It is so personal that I never even go there, because...it is that personal.*" I felt as though Piper had seen my life reviews, and that she saw where I had been. She offered an understanding and a knowing by trying to instill within me that I was capable of helping people in the face of death because of my personal experiences. I thought she must have seen some of my life events, but felt that it was so personal to me that she left it alone. She was sharing just enough insight with me that I would understand that she saw it, and that she knew it, and that I knew it too.

"*Also, the other part that makes that mystery with you is because of what you see. But, I want you to put the twist on it, put the beauty on it, put the love on it, and put the gift of the angels that are with you. I'm going to tell you that when you do this work, people that you are going to be with are going to look at you like you are the angel coming in. I'm just going to tell you that, because that's exactly how spirit is showing me. It's like they see you as an angel coming into the room, and sitting down with them, and talking with them. So, there is just hospice written all over you...okay. But, you can do with it whatever you want. This is the real nurturing in you, it's the nurse in you, and it is very natural.*"

After the reading was complete, questions started flooding out of my mouth. I told her that I had seen colors around people for years, I wanted to know what it was, and was there something wrong with me. She told me that it was spiritual sight and that I saw the energy around people. She told me that the colors are a person's aura. I told her about the visions I have when I come into close proximity to people. She told me that I was a true spiritual medium, and that I had the gift of automatic writing...I had no idea what that was so I wrote it down on a scrap piece of paper. She told me that it was a form of channeling, people write what spirit talks to them about. Well, that explained a lot for me. When I was a little girl between five and six years old, sometimes my mom would take me to the hospital with her where she worked. The nurses would give me a clip-board with paper and pen so I would have something to occupy my time and I would sit for hours and write. It relaxed me, and it just felt comfortable. I would write perfectly on the lines, sometimes I would fill twenty or more of the sheets of paper that looked like scribble to me, but it also looked a whole lot like cursive writing. I remember one day one of the sweet nurses came up to me and asked me what I was drawing so I showed her, she picked up the clip-board and flipped through the pages with interest and handed it back to me with a peculiar look on her face. I always wondered what I had done wrong. Looking back on that I have to wonder if she knew that it was automatic handwriting. I don't know if it scared her, or amazed her.

Piper told me that everything was going to be okay, and that I could relax. She said that all of the answers to my questions would come to me. She told me that it would be brought to me in the form of books. She said that there were many books that had the answers to my questions. As I was walking out her door, she revealed that she felt that a friend of mine would give me a book. I gave her a hug and said goodbye, knowing that somehow, I would see her again someday. I felt a genuine connection to her soul. Visions flooded my head of times we would be together in the future. I shut the door behind me and walked down the steps towards my friend waiting for me.

My friend smiled at me and asked me how my reading went—she wanted to know if I had had a good experience. I was still amazed by all that had been revealed to me, and I told her that the reading was very eye opening, and that Piper was quite accurate. I told my friend that Piper knew things about me that I had never told a single soul. My friend smiled and told me she was very happy that I had a good experience. She told me that during my reading she went into the bookstore and purchased some books. She handed me a book about auras...I looked at her in amazement and told her that Piper told me that my friends would be giving me books to help me understand myself. As I looked at the cover of the book, I stood in silence, engulfed with a reverence of newness and peace. Finally, I had some of the answers to what I was searching for, my life was beginning anew. The path less traveled now had my footprints.

Chapter 2

First Sight ~ Opening the Eyes

Something happens to a person when they surrender and let the soul come in and guide them. The true purpose is revealed and the mind, the ego is no longer running the show. When we allow this transformation to take place, life turns into a whole new dimension. I had been pushing against the flow of life for so long that my logical mind and my personal fears ran the show, and it was a complete failure. Finally, I had an explanation of what I thought was wrong with me, and it was as if I were coming to life for the first time. I had spent years resisting…trying to shut out all that was me. The problem was that I did not realize what I was doing—I would fight so hard to be in control of what was going on around me that my internal battle became a way of life. The anger that I had built over the course of many years had engulfed my soul and it shrouded who I was to the core. The layers of mistrust had built a wall around my soul to the point that I could only live in solitude. The only thing that seemed to bring me to life during this time was my fear, anger and sadness. Then there were the quiet times of my depressions where I sank lower and lower, coming up occasionally to try and be a hero and fix everything around me. I knew it all. I had earned my wisdom, or so I thought. This was the misconception, the failure and the beginning of my lessons this time around on the earth.

After the meeting with Piper, I opened my heart to a truth that I had been trying to hide from all of my life. I was hiding from my spiritual gifts, and my ability to see the things in the spaces in-between. These things were spirits, earthbounds, and angels, and many other things that quite frankly, I had no understanding of what they were. Because of my ignorance of these things unknown, and the fact that they scared me, my spiritual sight along with my physical eyes had become blurred and fuzzy. Consequently, my gift of feel had intensified. This is not unlike the person who suddenly loses sight and becomes blind—thereby creating a heightened awareness of the other senses. This can be very uncomfortable when dealing in the world of spirit and energies. I felt as though most of the time I was in a dense forest whereby I could feel the fear, frustration, and anger. It was right next to me, it was in me, but I couldn't see it. Therefore, my tremendous fears would block my spiritual sight. All it would take would be one glimpse of the spirit and as a defense mechanism my spiritual sight would shut immediately leaving me with these tremendous feelings of fear. When Piper told me in my reading that in the future I would be helping people crossover and that I would help them make peace with their lives, her understanding of my gifts gave to me my soul's purpose. I was opening my eyes, and my soul was awakening. Everything that seemed so scary and strange about me started to make sense.

The drive back home from Cassadaga that day was filled with feelings of exhilaration and fear. What would my family think of me if I told them what Piper told me? What did I think? I was always my own worst enemy in the ways of my internal truths. I wanted to speak the truth, but it was always so hard to find the words that would make some sort of sense, therefore my default was to simply keep it to myself. Deep down, I knew that this was the day that I would be coming out of the closet, and I felt scared and liberated both at the same time. This had been the roller coaster of my life. I had always thought that something was wrong with me, and now a part of me felt that my fears of being an oddball had been validated. I was not normal in the normal sense of the world...or was I? Most of the things that happened to me *I* had a hard time believing. So, how was I to expect that anyone else would believe the strange occurrences? These things had happened to me! How was I supposed to tell of my experiences with a straight face knowing for myself that it was hard to believe? Strange as all of the emotions felt, and they were both high and low, there were also energies of calm and exhilaration flowing through my being.

By the time I got home I was anxious to re-listen to the recording of my reading. There was a part of me that wondered if I had heard her correctly... I wondered if I had imagined the words out of her mouth—*stranger things have happened*. I was grateful that I did not have to rely on my memory, and that I had thought to record the session. I greeted my family and then almost immediately went out to the back porch with my recorder in hand. I put the tape into the machine and listened to it intently. There was much that I had missed hearing during the reading and some of what I heard was new material for me. After awhile, Luke joined me on the back porch and asked if he could listen to the reading. I was surprised that he was interested in hearing the tape. I had not yet discussed what the reading was about with my family.   The uncomfortable truth was that I had a hard time finding words to explain myself.   I simply never really understood what it was I was experiencing, and because of my fears I never explored and tried to learn about myself.   Deep within I had a fear of learning about myself. I did not want to learn that I was crazy, so I hid from myself. I stopped the tape and talked with Luke for a little while explaining some of the things that I experienced such as colors around people. I told him that this was spiritual sight and that I had learned from Piper that the colors are called a persons aura.   It was fun to watch his reactions to the reading. He was so interested and intrigued by what was said about the hospice, and helping people make the transition to the other side. Savannah joined us on the back porch but her enthusiasm was limited to a few minutes.   The next morning when David returned home from work we talked about the reading, and he listened to the tape. He was very supportive and he thought it was great that I had fun with my girlfriend.

The days and weeks that followed my meeting with Piper were full of reading and researching, and all that I could learn about the spiritual realms. The deeper I dug for information, the more questions about me surfaced and I could not seem to learn enough. For the first time in my life I did not feel alone. I was astounded at the numbers of people out there who were just like me. It was awesome. I read all I could find at my public library, I started learning about meditation for the first time in my life, and I purchased many cd's to help me meditate. I found my "*center*" and loved it so much that meditation became a daily routine.   It is interesting how much I had changed and surrendered, because I used to think that people who meditated were strange—I would roll my eyes at the thought of them meditating. How little I knew. Having learned so much about me in such a short time was truly enlightening, and I was soaking it all in with a song in my heart.

I soon discovered that when a person opens up, it has a profound effect on the others around you. They feel the energy—and with the knowledge coming forth it also allows them to dispense of their fears as well. It opens a gateway to the world of spirit. Luke and Savannah were already on the road that I had traveled many years alone, they had the gifts, and I did not know it. I laugh about it now, but when I asked Savannah why she did not tell me about the things that she had seen, her response to me was; *"Why didn't you tell me about the things that you saw?"* She got me there!

One evening shortly after David went to work I went into my bedroom to listen to a guided meditation from one of my new cd's. Luke and Savannah had been watching tv and after a while they found their way into my room. The both of them snuggled into the bed under the covers next to me. The music on the meditation recordings can be quite relaxing—I think the beautiful sounds were what drew the kids into my room. As was the case many times before, I fell asleep during the meditation. I awoke suddenly to the sound of Luke's voice. He was smiling ear to ear and literally glowing, he was so happy. He told me that he had just met his spirit guide Elijah, and that he had seen him clearly. He said *"Mom, just like I see and talk to you!"* He was talking fast and with great enthusiasm. He described his guardian angel as having silver hair and silver wings, and that when he took a breath it was as if he breathed in the angel's breath. He said it felt like cool and humid, and the breath gave him feelings of great joy. He said it was so cool. Savannah had a similar experience and was very happy too, although, Luke's excitement was off the charts!

That moment in time, the meditation with the kids did profoundly change all of our lives. Many times I have heard people say that God works in mysterious ways. However, my experience has been quite the contrary. I now believe that when God wants it done, *it is done immediately*! The days that followed the meditation with the kids, Luke began talking to grandpa and his spirit guides. It flowed naturally for him. Out of nowhere he was giving me readings, and telling me about my past lives...the words just fell into his mind and right out of his mouth. It was astonishing! His soul was wide open and ready to receive messages from spirit, and it was a beautiful experience to behold. Savannah's third eye opened so fast that we all had whiplash. She could see all of the spirits, angels, and earthbounds very clearly. It was like a whirlwind. This all happened so fast that I did not know what to think. Thoughts of doubt and self sabotage started to creep into my being. I started to think that I had somehow brought my kids into a wacky world that I had still not fully accepted. I thought many times to myself that it was bad enough when I thought I was nuts, now I was bringing my kids with me.

Strange events started progressing rapidly in our home. It was as if we had opened a portal to the world of spirit. We were all diving in full speed ahead and the energy in our home was exciting, yet unknown. It is hard to put into words how our lives evolved and opened at this time in our life, and I was not the only one who was opening up to the acknowledgement that life was more than we had experienced for years. I remember thinking to myself that it was a good thing that I was ignorant to all things in the world of spirit as I had no formal rules. We did not come into this life with a guide book to help us through these strange times. I was diligent in trying to find as many answers as possible. However, there was nothing in any play book that fully described what was happening to us. If I had been scripted towards some of the events that came into our life, I think I would have messed them up by imposing too many rules upon what should and shouldn't be. Our experiences were new and unknown territory for us—not unlike what it must be like for scientists who are trying to explore new discoveries. For us, we were in unchartered territory.

One night as I was asleep on the couch, Savannah came out of my bedroom and woke me with a scared look on her face. She told Luke and me that she saw something in my room. I told her to go back into the room and look again. She came running out of my bedroom and told us that she saw a little girl with brown frizzy hair. I kept my poker face on so she would not be afraid and told her that it was okay. Internally, I was trying to deal with the fact that Savannah could see these things, and I knew personally how scary it could be—I think it was because of my opening up, and sharing with her that in some way it made it real for her too. Therefore, true to form, I decided to play it off like it was nothing. I told the kids not to worry about it, and the best thing to do would be to ignore the little girl, and that maybe she would go away, then I fell back to sleep. About an hour later Luke was playing video games on the computer while Savannah watched. The little girl came back and stood next to Savannah. While Savannah was watching the games she noticed in her peripheral vision the little girl creeping up slowly to the side of her face. The little girl had figured out that Savannah could see her. Excited to finally be seen, the little girl went a little further, she put her lips together and made a loud popping sound in Savannah's ear. Luke woke me to tell me what had happened. I told the kids that we would deal with it in the morning, and there was nothing to worry about. I told them that we needed to get some sleep, so we went to bed. I was too tired to deal with the dead.

Savannah slept with me that night, and the next morning the three of us went to the back porch to talk about what had happened the night before. I do not smoke in my house, so that seemed to be the gathering place to talk. The cigarettes grounded me in a strange way—they gave me something to hold on to, as I had used cigarettes for years as my only friend. Together we decided that we needed to cross this little girl over to the light. Since my recent education on all things spirit, I had discovered that these "*ghosts*" were simply earthbound people that needed to go through the light to get home to heaven. We all decided that the best thing to do would be to try and find the little girl. Therefore, reluctantly Savannah went into the house in search of our little earthbound visitor. I convinced Savannah that the best way to deal with the situation was to talk the little girl into going home to heaven. I think she agreed because it was daylight and she did not want to experience any more late night intrusions. Savannah found the little girl in her bedroom and told her to come to the back porch so that we could talk to her, the little girl agreed and followed Savannah outside. This was a fly by the seat of our pants situation as we had never done this before. We invited the little girl to sit down because we wanted her to feel as comfortable as possible. Savannah drew a picture of the little girl while we all talked with her. She seemed to like the attention that we gave to her. We were all confused as to what to do, so we struggled through and talked to her about whatever she wanted to talk about. We kept telling her that she was okay, and that it was time for her to go to heaven. The little girl was happy to hear that she could indeed go to heaven. Savannah helped her by showing her the white light, I think that was an important validation to the little girl that Savannah saw what she saw. We also asked for her family members from the other side to come and help her go home, I think it was her grandma who came and took her home. This was the beginning, she was our first earthbound success story, and we were relieved that it went so well…that she actually crossed over. When I told my husband about it later he was bit ambivalent about the situation. He was worried, admittedly, as was I. We were stepping into new and unknown territory and it was somewhat unnerving. It was one thing to read about these things, but an entirely different situation to experience them first hand. I remember thinking that I felt as if I were in the twilight zone. Selfishly, I wanted the little girl to cross over so that we did not have to deal with anymore late night surprises. Quite frankly, I was trying to get rid of her. I was not trying to be any kind of cool person, I simply wanted her to go away and this was the only answer I had thus far.

A few nights after the little girl incident Luke and Savannah decided that they wanted to have a slumber movie night in the den. The kids pulled out the couch bed so they could watch movies all night. David and I had fallen asleep in our bed when Savannah came to me and woke me, and she was very upset. She told me that Luke was asleep and that there was a man trying to turn on our computer in the living room. While she was watching tv she heard a loud noise coming from our front door, and then she saw a shadowy figure running down the hall into the living room, anyone could imagine that she became very frightened. She said that when she finally worked up the courage to run into my bedroom she ran as fast as she could. I saw that she was very scared as her face was pale, and I could feel Savannah's fear because it penetrated my body like a wave of pins and needles. Mama bear kicked in and I knew that I would do anything to help her feel better. I left my room and we found that he was no longer in the living room by the computer so we went into the den in search of him—our late night intruder. I must admit, I was a bit cranky and could not wait to have words with this man who scared my little girl. Something happens to me when I feel fear, regardless if it is mine, or someone else's—I get very angry, and have a tendency to lash out towards the person who caused the fears. We found him in the den standing by the television. I asked Savannah if the guy she saw was an older gentleman with a white t-shirt and light colored slacks—she confirmed my observation. He seemed harmless enough to me and I got the distinct impression that he was confused and surprised that we could see him and that our acknowledgement of him had left him speechless. Rather quickly the anger drained from my being and was replaced with compassion. I remember distinctly that he felt so alone, and scared—his emotions were strong which explained why Savannah was experiencing so much fear, she could feel his fear. Those who posses the gift of feel must first ask the question *"Who is wrong with me?"* I had learned that when you possess these gifts you feel what others feel, and this is the first bridge of communication. We asked him what his name was and as far as we could tell it was Irwin. I told him that he was scaring my daughter and that he was dead, and that he needed to go to the light. I did not mince words—I got straight to the point. I am sorry to say that I can get pretty grumpy with earthbound spirits that aggravate me in the middle of the night. The strangest thing was that he just stood there and stared at us, so I told Savannah that we just needed to go to bed. We went to my bedroom and got into bed, she snuggled in next to me and my husband. As I was dozing off to sleep I woke with a start, it felt as if my soul had been jerked from my body for a split second. Someone had turned the computer on in the living room and the blue light of the screen was reflecting on my bedroom door. For some reason I became scared and just froze. I did not move a muscle. I knew it was the old man. I was so glad to have Savannah and David in the bed next to me. For a second I considered waking her, but then my senses came back to me and I realized that I did not want to wake my baby girl because she had finally gone to sleep. I remember wondering what in the hell was happening to my life and my children. This was not cool and I wanted it to stop. I started to get the feeling that things would not be normal for a while. Eventually my mind and heartbeat slowed down enough so that I could relax. As I had many times in my childhood, I stayed frozen in my bed in terror for about an hour before I drifted off to sleep.

The next morning Savannah and I told Luke and David what had happened to us the night before. Luke was willing to try and get more information for us, and he did. Luke learned that Irwin had died of a heart attack while being mugged outside of a court house in some town in Georgia. Irwin was confused because he did not know that he was dead. He just seemed to pop into our house that night. After Savannah and I had gone to bed he decided that he was going to access his email account on my computer, but he was only able to turn the monitor on creating more confusion for the poor old man. He was in his late sixties and had worked as a stenographer at the court house. The guy that robbed him took off with his wallet. The incident scared

Irwin so much that he had heart failure and died on the spot. We talked to Irwin about what had happened to him, we were kind and patient as he was not the kind of guy that wanted to be rushed. He was a silent man and a thinker, I got the distinct impression he was mulling over the words that we spoke. We told him that everything was going to be okay. It was interesting, because as we talked and listened, I think that it was somehow therapeutic for him. The process also opened his heart to the fact that he was dead, but not dead...as I always say. Finally, he crossed over through the light and went home. We learned something new that day through Irwin. We came to understand that he did not know that he was dead and because of that he was earthbound. I think he must have felt that he was experiencing some sort of weird dream, so he went along with it. It wasn't until we started talking directly to him that he started to realize the realness of what had happened to him. He did what he did so well in his life...he thought about it long and hard then came to the realization that he was not in his body any longer. It was helpful that we were able to help him remember his last moments in front of the courthouse. Once he started to remember the event that led to his demise, it all started to make perfect sense to him...in that thought it seemed as though he lifted himself from the fog of doubt.

In his own words—here is Irwin's story:

"I wandered around my city and home for awhile and then I found myself at your home looking into the eyes of a horrified little girl. I just stood there and stared at her—we stared at one another. She ran out of the room and then came back with you. I listened carefully to the conversation that y'all had together. I know you told me I was dead. Because of that

and the interesting state of mind I was in, for some reason I thought that I could email my wife from your computer and tell her that it was my time to cross over and go to heaven (as you put it too me). Although, I was able to turn your monitor on, I was unable to get signed into my email. That was very frustrating to me. So, I hung around your home until you woke in the morning. I kept trying to tell you to email my wife, but no one seemed to hear me. All y'all kept saying to me was 'go home, you're dead but not dead!' and 'go through the white light its heaven.' Y'all were a damn broken record (my opinion at that time). In fact you told me that nothing else mattered and that once I went home I could come back to my wife and help her. When you told me that I could do that—that was when I made the decision to go home to heaven. Thank you for helping me to 'see the light'."

Irwin also shared a little about his life with me:

"I really like the color red. My favorite time of year was fall. I was married for over thirty years to the same woman. We had three children, 2 daughters and one son. I was a jack of all trades for some time. I adventured out to find my way. I came from humble beginnings and left this earth with humble means. I died before my wife died. I really did not know that I was dead. My reality was mixed and confused—it felt real, yet not real. I was a quiet sober man in life, very few saw me, I kept quiet and to myself. So when I was a wandering spirit it was not different than my physical existence. I kept thinking about all of the chores that I needed to do. I was a list and project person. When I did not know I was dead my mind operated in the same fashion as it did while I was alive. It continued unbroken. I kept feeling and wanting to complete my list. The last conversation I had with my wife was about the leaves that I needed to rake up in the *yard. We had a fuss over this before I left for the day as I had been putting it off for quite a while. So, I kept thinking about the fact that I needed to get home to rake the leaves from the yard. When y'all told me I died from a heart attack I did remember all at once, yet the act itself was like a black-out to me, a memory erase. That is why I had no recollection of the incident in front of the court house. I guess you could have thought I had PTSD* (post traumatic stress disorder*) I blanked the moments of my death out of my memory. My favorite candy was caramel squares although they always gave me heartburn, I ate them anyway. I never really settled on a career, I did this and that. I had a lot of different jobs. I wasn't reckless or irresponsible, I just liked to learn how to do everything. I worked in a lot of trades—I drove my wife nuts! She worked (*as far as I could understand Irwin at this point because it became a bit fuzzy when he would talk about his wife I think she was some sort of book keeper or worked in a library or somewhere there were lots of books and records. She kept track of something.) *My wife always wore an apron over her clothes when she was home and she always wore some sort of hair net or hair cap to keep her hair in order, and she always wore lipstick. She did a little college before we married. In my life I learned how to tap dance I also sang in a barbershop quartet at one time. I was stubborn about going to the doctors when I fell ill and sometimes I was careless and did not take my medications. Everyone knew of my heart condition, it really was not a surprise to anyone that I died of a heart attack."*

At this point in time many things were changing around us so quickly that it was hard to think straight. We had many moments in this time that were quite unnerving. Savannah had begun to struggle with her gift of sight and because she knew that it was real, she starting going through some frightening moments as does anyone with these gifts. We spent many hours talking about what she had seen through the course of her young life. Luke and Savannah both came out of the closet and told me about people that they had seen that looked see-through. This was nothing new, only now they had an outlet to speak their truths. This is the sort of thing that when it happens to a person, when a person can see spirits and earthbounds, it is kept hidden within the dark corners of the mind. It is not something that you want to tell anyone because you feel that maybe there is something wrong with you. There is a fear within that others will think you are going crazy. As a natural defense these experiences are kept deep inside and it becomes second nature to push away anything that you might see—*or shouldn't see.* It is only when you talk with others, and receive validation that you can begin to accept that it is really happening.

Suffice it to say that all we had experienced thus far was trial and error. I wanted to prove to myself that all of these things were real, so one day while I was in my kitchen I saw a lady who was in her mid fifties, she had red hair and wore a cream colored shirt. I wanted to know if I was delusional or not, so I called Savannah into the kitchen and asked her if she saw anything in the room. She told me that she saw a woman in her fifties with red hair with a light colored shirt. That experience was eye opening for me, offering the validation that one would naturally seek in times like these... and believe me when I say, these little instances when you are hanging on by a thin thread truly do help with ones state of mind. I knew that there was no way possible that Savannah could have made it up—she was so accurate in describing to me the same person that I saw. That moment gave me what I needed in my heart and soul. In the past when this happened to me, I would doubt myself, fearing that I was delusional and just making things up in my mind. I had tried so hard to hold on to what Piper told me for validation, I just need something more concrete. I searched for something for me, and I got it through Savannah's eyes. I think that experience helped Savannah as well. She seemed to accept her gifts as more natural and a part of herself rather than a curse. Even though she was advanced in the ways of accepting her gifts, she did have experiences that scared her. The only difference was, now I was aware of her fears, and could help her through them. She told me that there were many nights in the past that she laid in her bed in terror. She had been afraid to come and tell me about what she had seen because she thought she was going crazy. She would always find her way into my room, and we would start to talk about random things and then we would fall to sleep. I think it was a good thing that I let her sleep in my bed whenever she wanted. Think about this...this fear was happening to a little girl all alone and she actually thought she was nuts.

I was thankful that I had opened my heart in acceptance of my spiritual gifts, because now neither one of us was alone. Talking openly about our experiences was healing and we were both able to work through our fears together. I know from personal experience that no one wants to go through this alone. It was now possible for her to be openly afraid, she did not have to hold it in any longer. Luke, on the other hand did not have the gift of sight like Savannah, although he would have the visions. Mostly his gift was communicating with spirit, and he was having a blast with his gifts. He was our portal to truth and information. His channel was wide open and he did not have any fear like Savannah or I, so he acted as our anchor. It was comforting to us that he was able to explain in great detail what was happening. Luke had established a wide open communication with his spirit guide and grandpa, and they were very happy and willing to give us all the information that we were seeking.

During the course of this time, the time of acceptance of our gifts, we were going through many emotional highs and lows. We were in a land of not knowing what the hell we were doing— we were going off of the cuff, doing the best we could with what we knew. Many times I would worry about Luke and Savannah. There were even times that I felt a deep guilt for giving them life, a life that was seemingly cursed. I would think to myself that if only they had come into this existence with another mother they would not be facing this crazy and scary life. Life for my husband was becoming increasingly difficult and I think that on some level he was full of fear for his children. It was extremely difficult for him to stand by and watch Savannah being scared, and he felt helpless. He had a hard time talking about what we saw so we started to keep it between the three of us as much as possible. It was too much for him to digest in such a short period of time and I understood why he felt the way he did. However, I was not about to force my kids back into the closet to make it any easier on him, and I was not going to go back into the darkness of hiding what happened to me either.

It was comforting that I had the kids to talk to about what I saw, and I know it was comforting for them as well. We were there to offer support to one another, and even before I learned of the term through reading spiritual books and websites Savannah told me that we were what are called "white-lighters" or "light-workers". This seemed to happen to us a lot through the course of trying to figure out what was happening. We learned that the truth was the truth, and it was always consistent. I would hear something from spirit, the guides or the angels—incidentally Luke and Savannah would hear it too, and then I would find the validation about a week later in a book. It was nice to find the answers in the books. However, I remember questioning why they (our angels and spirit guides) wouldn't just give it to me through the book in the first place. Their answer to me was clever—they told me that I would believe the truth coming to me this way, that somewhere in my mind if I found it in the book first and then I heard it from spirit, I would go to a place in my mind where I would think that I made it all up because I had read it first in a book. They told me that I would not have believed in what was happening to us, had I not heard it from spirit first. The spiritual realms were working hard to help us find the validations that we were seeking. Deep within I knew there was great wisdom in the ways that spirit allowed things to unfold before us. The answers always seemed to appear just in time, I guess you could say our answers came in "Divine Timing!" We worked very hard to find the answers and I documented everything we heard—*I call it the bread crumb trail*. It was interesting because I would write something down not thinking much of it at the time and then later I would find that it fell into place, and made perfect sense. It was almost as if we were fitting pieces of a puzzle together. I call all of these events organized chaos. During this period of time we were not only opening our spiritual eyes, we were literally opening our eyes to the eternal truths of the universe.

Chapter 3

The Spaces In-between and Within

Do you ever wonder what are in the spaces in-between? Living in this existence as I have for so many years I have grown to accept the things that I see in the spaces in-between as just what it is. What I mean by accept is this: They are always there, and there is nothing I can do about it...they remain there no matter how often I have wished that they just disappear. These are the things that I have seen that are there, but do not appear to be there. It has left me feeling helpless, scared, and at times completely crazy. I coped with this by training my eyes to try and look past these things. I would try and focus upon what seemed to be solid, such as a wall, or a sofa. These beings, objects and visions cannot be validated, and I have accepted that. When a person is born seeing these things, they learn through experience that others may not see them. It is something that becomes secret and silent. Perhaps it is as normal as growing up with the knowledge that the sky is blue, and the grass is green. However, the color of the sky and grass has reached a consensus and what a person with spiritual sight sees, has not. It is simply a gift that is intangible.

Our life was beginning to fill with turmoil each day as we started discovering more and more earthbound spirits and it was becoming increasingly difficult for me to try and do it on my own. I needed some guidance and direction. I needed help with my kids from someone who was familiar with the world of spirit. I was desperate to find answers—it had been one thing for me to live within the quagmire of own my existence—however, now it was affecting my children and I knew that I had to take some action. It was becoming more difficult as each day passed in this period of time to find a sane moment. It was as if spirit had taken over our lives. The earthbound spirits kept coming into the house, and each time we would cross them over. Hence, it started to feel like a duty. Every time that I wanted to say no, I would unconsciously energetically connect with the lost soul and feel overwhelmingly guilty—therefore, I would stop what I was doing and I would talk to the person and help them cross over through the light. It was turning into a daily ritual…one that was becoming increasingly frustrating.

In the past I had worked hard to tune out what was going on around me in the spaces in-between. However, now I could not do that because Savannah would come to me in fear and needed my help. Because she saw so clearly, the earthbound spirit would realize that she could see them, hence, they would follow her around and not leave her alone, leading her to come to me for help. We would sit out on the back porch and Savannah would draw a picture of the person…they seemed to like that attention, I think it grounded the earthbound in a way of allowing them to open their hearts to accepting what we were trying to convey to them. Grandpa and spirit would talk through Luke and I would be given the information to tell the person what they needed to hear in order for them to cross over. I would receive feelings of which I would convey to them, such as, their arm hurt or that I knew the person was crying. They were seeking validation of who they were and we did everything we could to help them realize that they and we were indeed real. In the meantime as this was happening I would frequently try and talk to my husband about what was happening around the house. He was having a very difficult time of it because he did not see the things that we saw and he could not do anything to help us. He felt as if his hands were tied and at times he was angry at the earthbounds for being in his house. I was becoming frustrated as well because I was starting to feel that I did not have any control over my surroundings. We were desperate to do the right thing, but I really did not know what the right thing to do was, I was literally taking it one moment at a time. I kept thinking that each time would be the last, each time I would help a person cross over I would have a second of satisfaction followed with the fear of more to come. That fear was validated because there never seemed to be a last person...there was always another one.

The spirit activity gradually started to increase, it went from one a day, and then the next day we would have two, and it peaked at about three a day. Opening our home and hearts to help those in the spaces in-between created an avalanche of beings into our lives. We soon discovered that when we went out to the store or shopping we would inevitably bring them home with us. Throughout my life I had learned to ignore the beings in the spaces in-between. However, Savannah's gifts were at a peak, and in a way, because she was so acutely aware, the earthbound spirits were attracted to her. Through time and experience I learned that anytime I had inadvertently looked at or felt the presence of an earthbound spirit, and they realized that I noticed them, they would get excited and then they become what

I call hitch-hikers. They would follow us around the store and then join us in our car. At first we would allow them to come home with us so we could cross them over, but that quickly became inconvenient because if we were not done shopping for the day they would tag along. It got to the point that when we stopped at a red light or stop sign we would tell them to go through the light. *Most of them do not like to cross over while going 55 mph in a car.* I know that looking at this situation from afar, it would seem like extremely odd behavior, and if one were to stand in judgment of my decision making for the most part a person might view my behavior as really out of this world. I had a feeling that this possible assertion by others would be hard for me to dispute for I felt like I was in some sort of wacky world myself. In so many ways I felt helpless, and yet I realized that these earthbounds were real people too. I just couldn't turn my back on the lost souls. In a way I felt like an air traffic controller directing the lost souls to the runway light, to a safe landing to the other side!

Anyhow, it would be an understatement if I were to say that this activity was consuming our lives, and I did not like that I was not in control of my surroundings. I wanted to get back to the normality of our existence, to the way it had been before the earthbounds started increasing in our home. Nonetheless, I was accepting of Luke and Savannah's gifts and I wanted to support them so they would not feel uncomfortable about themselves. From my own experiences of feeling like a misfit, I knew that it was important to accept the gifts of my children. However, there was a part of me that was mad at God for making them this way. I thought it was too much for a child to bear, I thought it was too much for me to bear in my own childhood. I kept telling myself that it was better for my children because they had me to help them through this and that I had experience with this sort of thing, so it wouldn't be so bad for them. I did my best to shield my children from their fears, I would console them and tell them that there was nothing wrong with them, but I really did wish that it would go away. *This was a tricky situation*. The last thing in the world I wanted was for my children to feel like there was something wrong with them, so in an attempt to prove to them that they were not crazy, I helped the souls as they came in and I tried to make it seem as normal as possible for my children—for me the easiest way to do that was to act like it was not a big deal, and that we just needed to let the lost soul know that they needed to go to heaven. Even with all of my doubts, I had a deep knowing within my heart that I had tapped into the purpose for which I had been searching for all of my life. It was right in front of me the whole time. The part of me that I was desperately trying to escape was the reason for my existence. The experiences that I had throughout my life and the things that I saw were there for a reason. I had a job to do, and for years I ran away and cursed my gifts. It was no wonder that I had felt so out of sync with my life.

Through time, I had learned to reluctantly accept that we cannot choose who we are once we get into this existence, it is already done...these are the spaces within. The spaces within are who we are at a core level. But, for me it was a hard pill to swallow, and I was angry and bitter much of my life at who I was. The anger was turned within and then towards all who were around me. I lashed out, and whoever was around me at the time felt my wrath. I know that I am not alone though, because many of us have fits over our own type of existence. We go through a rebellion of who we are for many years denying and trying to change all that we are. We feel as though we are stuck to a certain extent, and there are some things that we simply cannot change. Dreaming for a change or ignoring who we are will not make it disappear. We can choose to ignore who we are and we can even run from ourselves as I had for many years. However, the results of our denial are horrible because then that is when everything seems to go wrong, our lives become a walking misery. Every one of us experiences this at one time or another during our lives.

My natural ability to see into the spaces of the in-between was what I was running away from. My gifts did offer up my purpose to what my life's work could naturally be. However, my gifts had become useless as I ran away from my uniqueness in search of something that I was not. I wanted to be anything other than what I was, and it was a crash and burn. It did not serve me well to run away from my within…because, these were my natural gifts and abilities. We are all born into certain and different circumstances. Some of us are born without a father, some of us are born with white skin and sea blue eyes, others of us are born with cocoa colored skin and brown eyes. It is just the way we are. We are the beauty of The Divine's expression. We are who we are for a reason, and the purpose could easily be revealed to us, if we but look at ourselves in a simple way. This simple knowledge if tapped into would offer a sea of answers. What of the person born without sight, or those who are born with a debilitating disease. It is just the way we come to this earth.

We are all unique to the ways of who we are, and many of us do not like nor accept what is. However, I think there is a hidden truth…one that we are guilty of trying to hide, that lies within our own uniqueness. I think that it speaks to our own personal missions for this earth life. If we were to open our eyes and hearts to the truth and to these clues of who we are, the within…they would eventually lead us to our own particular life purpose. If only we had the insight and the courage to accept and allow who we are to become as apparent, just as it is, we would solve a lot of our misery. Is it possible that it actually is supposed to be that easy? Is who we are if truth be told, too obvious? Must we seek and search under every rock to find ourselves? These are the gifts that come naturally to us. These are the gifts that we are born with. My husband was born an identical twin. Sometimes people would ask him what it was like being a twin and he would always respond to the person with; *"I don't know, what is it like not to be a twin?"* I think this was the most frustrating aspect of being a twin for him—people always asking him what it was like to be one. Also, when people would ask his parents or family about him, it was never *"How is David?"* it was *"How are Jon and David?"*, or *"How are the twins?"* It was as if people saw them as one person, not as individuals.

The person who is born blind can hear many things that a person born with sight does not hear. It would be natural that the blind person could teach us many things subtle and often unobserved. This would be their gift to us, this could be their purpose. The man born as an identical twin could offer the lesson to us that we are all unique, each and every one of us are different. The person born into poverty teaches us how to survive and to rise above, and can also offer a contrast for many who have more. Moreover, we all experience spiritual sight and sound from within. The person who is deaf does hear, and the person who is blind can see, it is called spiritual hearing and seeing…this is what separates the human body from the soul.

These are the spaces within that fill the gap of our existence on this physical plane. This is the place where we go to find the answers to unravel the mysteries of our divine life purpose. All of us really know to the core what we are here to do, we just don't like it sometimes, and it gets too hard.

Too much emphasis has been put upon the physical body. "Do I want to be buried or cremated?" This is a question that many people ponder over. The respect for the dead is so much about the care and how to dispose of the body—and rightly so. However, by not putting much thought into the fact that the body is a mere vessel, is the main reason why so many here on this earth become earthbound spirits. Their main enfaces in their life is of the physical and they forget to go within. A home that is abandoned no longer has a soul. The inhabitants of the home are what determine the feel and the energy within and around the physical property—it is the spirit and the soul of the people that give the home life and energy. There are many clues to the physical eye, looking at a home from the outside it is easy to see that the person likes to garden if there are beautiful flowers and plants surrounding the home. Some homes are cloaked with trees and there is no apparent way to the front door, this tells the casual observer that the person inside prefers solitude. The no trespassing signs will tell us to stay away. We all do things in a certain way, not even knowing why we do, so naturally, we seek help from others for answers. Sometimes, the answers could come easily from a complete stranger who is observant. This is why I am successful in helping earthbound people cross over to the other side. They need outside help. Much of who we are is so obvious, but we seem to miss what is right in front of our nose.

Because I was so embroiled in my situation, I too needed outside help. I needed someone who was not caught up in the emotion of our day to day living to give me some prospective for the situation. The person I needed to see who could offer me some outside prospective was Piper. After much frustration, one morning I woke up desperate and demanded answers. Therefore, I decided that we were going to go to Cassadaga. I was taking a huge leap of faith, but I did not care. I was filled with determination. I did not even know if Piper would still be in Cassadaga, for the last time I had contact with her was my first reading. Although, this did not stop me because I was on a mission from within, and I knew that I had to see her. I could feel that it was the right thing to do. On our way I left several messages on Pipers voicemail to let her know that I was coming into town, and was hoping that we could get a reading from her that day. By the time we arrived in the little town, I had not heard from her so I was full of anxiety. We went into the spiritualist bookstore to see if Piper was on the board and my heart sunk when I saw that she was not listed as one of the mediums taking readings for that day. I worried that maybe she was out of town, or that she was already booked-up for the day. The questions swirled around in my mind as I went to the counter to ask the lady tending to the store if she knew how I could get a hold of Piper. When I asked her about Piper, she told me that it was not unusual that she was not on the board. This was a surprise to me as my first reading from her came about because she was listed on that very board. I told the lady behind the counter that I desperately needed to see Piper that day and that I had traveled two hours but had been unable to make contact with her. The woman in the bookstore found another number that she had for Piper, it was her cell phone. I immediately tried it, but got her answering machine again. The realization was coming to me that I might not get to see her. I quickly began to question myself and my inner guidance as I had been certain that I was divinely guided to go to Cassadaga. I felt in my heart that I was supposed to see her—however it was beginning to feel as though I had been wrong in interpreting my guidance. Doubt sank in and I knew it that wasn't the first time I had been wrong.

The lady behind the counter told me that there were some really good mediums on the board that day. She offered to help me contact one to set an appointment for a reading. I told her an abbreviated version about my situation and that I needed to see someone with my two children, and that I would prefer someone who was good with gifted children. She told me that she had the perfect person. I thanked her for her assistance and asked if she would call for me, which she did. The medium said that she would be happy to see all of us together and that she could fit us in right away. Although I wanted to see Piper, I agreed to the reading, and set the appointment. I decided that we were there now, and if spirit was going to help us it could be through anyone. The thought occurred to me that maybe I was not supposed to see Piper that day, and I accepted that fate must be playing a hand in our situation. However, I was still very disappointed, and I held out hope that Piper would call me.

The woman in the store gave us the directions to the medium's house that we had just set the appointment with. My husband told me that it would be okay, and he reminded me that we were there for a reading, and that obviously we weren't going to get Piper because she was not home. I agreed with him, so we headed to our scheduled appointment to get our reading. When I spoke with the medium on the phone at the store I told her that I had tried to contact Piper with no success. She was very kind to me and was a sweet person— she assured me that there was nothing to worry about and that everything was going to be just fine and that she looked forward to meeting me and my two children.

On our way to her house we passed Pipers home. I kept staring at my cell phone commanding it to ring. *I knew that she would call me, I just knew it!* Even though we had an appointment set, I was still holding out hope that Piper would call me, and then I had a brilliant idea. In my mind I hollered out to grandpa, I called for him and I told him what I needed and that it was very important and that I was running out of time. I asked him to please contact Piper and tell her that I needed to see her. I held onto my phone and I think I was about to stare a hole in it when after what seemed to be the longest few minutes of my life the phone rang—I stared at the numbers surprise and grateful, it was Pipers number! I was relieved and said a quick thank you to grandpa and all those who helped. I answered the phone and asked her if she could see me with the kids. She told me that it was so interesting because she had just walked into her home from the store and she felt like she was supposed to go and check her answering machine. She heard my message, and was going to call me a in a little while once she was settled in from shopping, but something was urging her to call me right then. Her call to me was perfect timing as we were about to enter the driveway of the other mediums home. I explained to Piper that we had already set an appointment with another medium and told her that I did not want to create any problems for her, but that I wanted to cancel the other appointment. I told Piper who the woman was and she told me that she was a very kind and understanding woman, so I set the appointment with Piper and called the other woman who gracefully understood. She told me she was grateful for me that I was able to connect with Piper. I took a deep breath and my body relaxed. I was so grateful that I had been able to receive what I was in search of on that day. I was exhilarated and I felt that we were going in the right direction. When you have moments in your life that you just know that you have something that you have to do and you will not rest until you get it, this can be draining and then when you reach the point of success, it can be exhilarating. I knew that she had the answers that I had been seeking and somehow she could put some of this right and offer to me help for my children. My husband parked the car behind the bookstore, and I gave him a quick hug and told him we would be back in a little while. He told me not to worry about him because he could get some sleep in the car while we were at our appointment as he had worked the night before and was tired.

Piper greeted us with open arms and a smile. She gave all of us a warm hug and invited us into her sitting room. Once we settled into our seats I handed her the tape that I had purchased at the bookstore. As she prepared for the reading, the kids were looking around the room and Savannah noticed a picture of a grey wolf and pointed it out to all of us. We became excited and told Piper that over the last few days there had been a grey spirit wolf circling our home. She smiled as she told us that her spirit guide's name was Grey Wolf. We looked at one another with awe in our eyes. *Her spirit guide was using the animal spirit of grey wolf to tell us that he was moving things around for us in the universe...paving the way, and I knew that he was helping us so we could see Piper.* At that moment I had a realization that he had been working with Grandpa, and then it dawned on me that maybe we had a whole lot more help than we actually knew.

From that moment on whenever I see the grey wolf running around my house or have a vision of grey wolf, I know that I will have a connection with Piper of some sort. There have been times when I have felt lost and alone and the grey wolf has appeared to tell me that I was not alone, offering to me a gentle reminder that I did have many others helping me. The grey wolf is always one step ahead of me, because I will see him circling and think to myself that all is okay and that there really isn't a need to call or see Piper. However, within a few days I soon discover that the grey wolf was correct. There always seems to be a contact. I think it is pretty cool.

During the kid's first reading with Piper we tried to record the session, but the tape recorder kept shutting off, there was too much energy in the room, so we were not able to make a record of it. I was disappointed that we would not have a recording of our session, however I understood that I had received divine guidance leading us to Piper, so I accepted that if I was supposed to have the session recorded it would have been so. I had been trying to do that a lot...I was trying to accept that which I did not understand. I was learning how to be patient for the inevitable answer or sign that all was the way it was supposed to be.

Piper started the session by explaining to Luke and Savannah that they were not crazy because of the things that they heard and saw. She told the kids that there are some people on the earth that the veil separating them from the other side is very thin, allowing the person to see and hear spirits and angels. She told them that was the case for them. Almost immediately when Luke and Savannah sat at the table they were drawn to the beautiful stones and crystals that Piper had placed on the table around her. Piper noticed and handed them each a stone and started to explain some of the essences of the crystals and how the energies in each stone has a use and is helpful in healing. She talked to Savannah about the importance of crystals and that the crystal energies could help her feel more grounded and balanced. Piper told me that the bookstore had books that would explain the uses of the crystals and they also had crystals. Piper explained to me that it would be helpful for all of us to do research into them and use them, and that educating ourselves about the crystals and their properties would be a good start.

Savannah asked Piper why some of the earthbounds had certain colors around them. Piper explained to Savannah that if we were to put the color that she saw around the lost soul, it could help in healing the soul. She told us that there are always clues and messages to help us help others. Piper kept the reading very simple for the children, she was doing what I had hoped would happen—she was offering outside reassurances to them. Because of her experience in the realms of spirit she was able to show them that there are many other people who experience what they experience and that she herself was one of them. She told them the story of when her grandpa died, her family wanted her to go to the funeral but she did not want to because she could still see her grandpa's spirit. She was a little girl when this happened so I think it was helpful especially to Savannah to hear the story of Pipers childhood experiences. Piper reassured the kids that they were not alone and that there are many other children out there with the same gifts—and that they were indeed blessed and fortunate that they had understanding parents.

She talked to Savannah about her communications with the angels, telling all of us that we had plenty of help. She acknowledged that our connection to the angels is what helps us to feel safe and comfortable with the work that we do. She explained to us that it was important that we ask for help, and that the angels and others on the other side want to help us any way that they can. She reiterated that they cannot help us unless we asked for it. She said it was okay to ask for help in any area of our lives such as: money situations, parking spots, homework, and anything we felt we needed assistance with. She said that they are here helping us with our spiritual work, but that is not the only area of our lives that they can offer assistance. She told us that they are willing, ready and happy to help. She also told Luke about his science side and that in the future he would be interested in creating the technology so that everyone could see and talk to spirit. She told him that up until this point spirit had been whispering in his ear, but now grandpa was talking to him as clearly as she was. She explained to the children that these were beautiful gifts and that there was no need to fear. Piper made sure to tell the kids that they were not crazy or insane in anyway. She talked to them about some of the psychic children that lived in the Spiritualist Camp in Cassadaga and that it was accepted and a normal way of life for the kids to talk to spirit. She explained to them that she understood that it was very difficult living in the "real world" with these gifts and that the children in Cassadaga were blessed to be able to be open about which they truly are.

Piper went on to tell Luke and Savannah how blessed they were to have me as their mother with the understanding that I had. She complimented me on the fact that I was helping them come to terms with their gifts rather than shutting them off and that it was indeed a beautiful thing. She talked to us in great detail how important it was for us to have command over spirit and that we truly did have command. She told me that it was important to impose boundaries and limits upon the times that the angels could bring the lost souls to us. She even said that it would be a good idea if we were to tell them, "*Okay we will only do this on wed from 7-9, no more...*" She explained how important our intent was and that we needed to put boundaries and limits out to the universe as to what we would be willing to do. She was confident that it could be the way we wanted it to be, although I had my doubts, she reassured me that I must put my foot down and assert what I would and would not be willing to do. She did not want to see this overtake our lives and she counseled me that it was very important that I learn how to create a balance. She did understand that it had come in so fast and all at once, that I was struggling to keep my head above all that had been happening around me and that I felt as if I were drowning. She acknowledged the support that we had from my husband and that he just wanted us to be happy.

She reiterated how important it was to create balance in our lives and that balance would help us tremendously with my relationship with my husband. She explained how important it was to balance our physical earthly duties with our work with spirit. She counseled me that homework, laundry and shopping was just as important to our life as helping the lost souls. This was helpful to me because I never wanted to let God, the angels, or the earthbounds down. It was nice to hear from her that my personal life was just as important, if not more so than any of the other works that I do and that I needed to see to our physical, emotional and earthly needs as well as the other, *or more importantly our needs should always come first*. She told me this was the key for my husband, and that it would bother him extremely if he saw that the kids were not having a normal childhood as possible because of all of the spirit work. She counseled me that activities such as playing with other kids, homework, going to the pool and swimming should be the highest priority, and that if I dedicated our time likewise he would be okay with all of these new and uncertain things. She once again stressed the point that we needed to learn how to create a balance between the two worlds. She told me that he was also in the swirl of the events and it could leave him feeling helpless especially since he did not see, feel, and hear the same things that we did but that his purpose was to help keep us grounded in the physical world. She ended the reading by telling me that if I had any questions that I could call her anytime and to simply leave a message with *"it's me and the kids"* and she would know that it was me calling. I think that was the most important message for me because I had felt so alone and now I had someone with knowledge who I could go to in times of need. Before we left, she asked if we had any questions and one of the first things Savannah asked Piper was, *"Who is that guy standing next to you?"* Piper smiled and told her that he was her spirit guide Grey Wolf. Luke asked Miss Piper if his older brother Drew would be coming home soon. Drew wanted to live with my mom in Utah, David and I decided to allow him to do so. After about six months of living with my mom he went to live with my sister who also lived Utah. He had been gone for about nine months and we all wanted him to come home. Piper got a peculiar look on her face and told us that it would not be happening for a while because there were still things that Drew needed to experience, and that things were the way they should be. She told Luke that it would not be a good time for Jesse and Drew to be at the home right now because of all of the things that we were experiencing and trying to work through. She told us there would be a time that we would be together but that it was not to be anytime soon. We all nodded in agreement and there was a silent acceptance to the words that Piper spoke to us...we understood and we all knew that she was right.

The reading with Piper was complete and a beautiful energy permeated our beings in Piper's little sitting room. I felt at peace because of the reading and more grounded than I had in quite some time. It was helpful to my soul to receive the answers and guidance that we did on that day. We gave Piper a hug good bye and left to go to our car behind the bookstore.

As I walked up to the car David informed me that my sister had called and that I needed to call her immediately—I did call her right away and she informed me that Drew could no longer live with her. She told me that I needed to make arrangements for him immediately, so David called his brother who lived in a town an hour away from where Drew had been living and asked him if he could possibly go and get Drew. Thankfully he agreed. We were astounded because Piper had just finished telling us that Drew was not going to live with us for a while. Yet, moments after our reading I had a conversation with him and he was happy to come home. The events of talking with Drew lead us to doubt the validations that we had just received from Piper. *Talk about riding highs and lows—that was the case for this day*. Once again I began to feel as I was on emotional quick sand but I managed to keep my thoughts on the positive so I told the kids that regardless if Piper had misunderstood the information that she had been given, it had been a beautiful experience. They agreed with me and told me that they had a great time anyway, and that not everyone can be right all of the time. I just love the way kids view the world because they think on simple terms that are often the way to the truth. Our lows were accompanied with a magnificent high as we were all extremely excited that Drew was finally coming home. Unfortunately, we learned that Pipers revelations were accurate because when Drew came home he stayed with us for 30 hours before he told us he wanted to go and live with my oldest son, Jesse. We allowed him to do so, and once again our hearts were broken.

Since there was an awareness of so many of the spirit world around us in our existence, it made it easier for our communication that we defined who was who. Thereby, in our home we have an understanding of whom or what we are trying to communicate about with one another. Obviously angels are angels and there are a vast amount of different type's of angels in the angelic realms, including the fairies. I like to think of fairies as miniature angels with spunk. Their primary purpose is to help with Mother Nature...that is their domain, so to speak. However, the angels work with many others in spirit as well. Spirits are those souls who have made their transition and crossed over into the light, to Home, the other side, or Heaven, whatever you want to call our glorious place of existence in eternity. Ascended Masters or Masters as I often refer to them are highly evolved souls on the other side. They have lived many lifetimes and have much experience to offer help to those of us in the physical. One of the most well known Masters is Jesus Christ. Just know that there are many others like him helping us to evolve spiritually and grow. The Masters work closely with Mother and Father God and the Angels. Sometimes the masters will elicit the help of family members in spirit to help in a situation with a lost soul. Then there are the earthbound spirits, these are the lost souls who for some reason or another have chosen to stay on the earth for a time, rather than make their transition home to the other side. I liken it to a situation when you have had a falling out with your family and you chose to stay away for a time. The choice is always available for you to go home, it just happens when you are ready. The difference is that heaven is always waiting with love and support, while sometimes our earthly families are full of anger and resentment, and the later is often the fear that holds the lost souls in the earthbound state. Some of them carry within their being such disgust and guilt over their lifetimes that they fear condemnation from God. Therefore, much like we avoid some bad friends and family situations, they avoid dealing with God and those on the other side. There are also lost souls who walk the earth who are still in the physical body that are in need of help from the other side and they get the help much more than we all realize. The spaces in-between are also filled with spirit animals. These animals are pure and loving and they act as the same type of emotional buffer as our animals do in the physical realm. These loving beings are with us throughout our journeys upon this earth. The spaces in-between are filled with a host of heavenly helpers, so much so, that if your spiritual sight was fully awakened you would not be able to see past them. You would realize how full the spaces in-between are of heavenly helpers, and you would know that they are all with and around us at all times. They stand prepared and waiting to be asked for the help that you desire.

I learned many lessons on that day we went to see Piper. I learned that following guidance from within is often scary. I felt out of control because I could not see what was on our path ahead. I learned however, that those of whom we ask for help, particularly the heavenly helpers, can see the path ahead at a much further distance than we can. Following the guidance that they offer requires faith because logic often doesn't work.

Sometimes, when we try to use our logic we can get in the way of the help that we asked for and we then block it from our lack of willingness to see it through because it doesn't make common sense to us. I was grateful that our purpose in traveling to see Piper on that day did offer us a comforting feeling in our hearts, and because of our time with her we began the journey to accepting our gifts together. We started on the road to accept our experiences with the spaces in-between and within.

Chapter 4

Do You Feel What I feel?

One of the strongest spiritual gifts I was born with was the gift of feel, I am an empath. This means that I feel the energies of many beings on a deep, deep level. I discovered the full potential of my gift when I was in the presence of earthbound spirits who were in pain, be it physical or emotional—I felt the pain that they felt when they died. Through the course of time I learned that my gift of feel was the best source that I had to create a bridge of communication with the lost souls. True feelings never lie, and as an empath I naturally connected to the feelings, emotions and energies of the lost souls. I have grown to understand that earthbound spirits who were in pain when they died did not have the awareness that the event was over. The lost soul "carried over" the same pains, feelings and emotions into their earthbound experience as they did while they were in the skin, and it was one of the things that kept them in the earthbound state.

A way in which *we* can relate to the earthbound experience is through our own dream experiences. These are the dreams in which the world is upside down and crazy, yet we still play a part in the dream, going along with the "out of reality" events as if these experiences were the norm. In the strange dream there doesn't seem to be the realization that it is a dream-although it always feels as if something is desperately wrong. Whilst one is in these dreams it is hard to find the answers or a way to fix the problem, and sometimes it feels as if there will never be an escape from the wacky "reality". It is not until we awake from our slumber do we shake our head and wonder what the hell just happened.

Many times the only thing that seemed to snap the lost souls back to the here and now was when I conveyed to them the pain that they were feeling through my gift of feel. In other words, I was able to describe to them the exact pain that they were feeling because I felt it too. This communication would immediately grab their attention and it seemed to bring them out of their state of existence into to mine, into the here and now. It would "awake" them from their dream state.

During the first days of helping the lost souls, I started to use my gift of feel to my advantage…it was my spiritual tool of understanding and empathy. I also learned early on that once I connected to the energies of the lost souls who were in my presence, that I could not create a disconnect from their energies as long as they stayed in the earthbound state. (*I feel that it is quite possible that it was a "fail safe" that was a preplanned part of my soul's mission in helping the lost souls.*) Therefore, as long as they were in the earthbound state I would feel their pain and emotions because now we were connected…our energy was connected—seemingly as one. When I would talk to the lost soul I would explain our energy connection and when they learned this about me I seemed to gain much sympathy from the lost soul—especially if it were someone who was in a tremendous amount of pain. In these circumstances it would often become unbearable for me, therefore I would kindly ask the lost soul to *"go through the light- its heaven"* so I could heal their energies from my body. Because I was accurate in my account of what they were feeling, it seemed to offer to them the validation that what I was telling them was the truth, thus they felt safe to go through the light. This communication with the lost souls was a platform from which I could stand with great confidence. Therefore, it gave them a feeling of stability…which was necessary to them because they had felt so unstable for so long.

Once I was able to establish this bridge of trust, it created a situation whereby they believed me when I told them that they were safe and that the angels had brought them to me so that I could help deliver the message to them that it was time to go home and the way to do that was through the light. These experiences touched my soul on the deepest level, and gave to me the gift of witnessing the beauty of the eternal soul. For the first time in a long time they opened their awareness to the energies of love, and they felt compassion towards me. Because of this they did not want to be the cause of giving me physical pain! They were then able to change their way of thinking beyond their own suffering and pain—this was the key to a successful communication.

Communicating through the gift of feel with the lost soul wakes them up from their slumber and in a way I think it helps them to realize that they are not alone— they begin to understand that we are sharing the pain, the lost soul and I. In my conversations with them before they made their journey home I would explain to them that they had just taken a detour…the long road, but that they are safe now and it is simply time to go home. I felt as though I was blessed to be able to witness the true beauty of the pure soul and the essence of love when they thought of another other than themselves. It is a most beautiful gift to experience the mercy of a lost soul.

I learned how to cope with being an empath because I consciously acknowledged to myself that the pain I feel through the energies is simply a delusionary state, and through the power of thought all can be healed. I do have a knowing that because of the energies, to a certain degree the experience is real. In my logical mind I know this because I can feel—however I heed particular care to not allow myself to fall into the mind trap of the earthbound existence. In other words I do not own their pain...I use it as a tool to communicate. I work hard to keep the conversations to just the facts of the events of what happened to the soul. I keep it in my mind that this is now a past event and I am telling them their story. I open their minds to the reality of the now, and what was the past. It is always easier to view a traumatic event as a past event rather than the now, it is important to understand that the event has already happened. We often do this in the skin. So much of our lives are about tormenting our selves over what could have or should have been. When we allow the energies of past events to creep into our being this creates a situation whereby we do not want to let go of our pain. The pain becomes a friend of sorts. I think it has a lot to do with the fact that pain and suffering can become a way of life...a natural feeling if one lives with it long enough... it is habitual living. Once we come to realize that the past is the past, we can move forward and heal.

One day, out of the blue, my right hip felt as though it had been cut in half, and I literally had a hard time walking...so much so that my right leg kept giving out on me and on several occasions I almost fell to the ground. I searched in my mind to find the event that created my injured hip. This is the thing that happens to me a lot of the time. Even though I have the awareness that I am an empath, I often forget that what I am feeling might be coming through the energies from someone else. Incidentally, it matters not whether the person is alive or dead, the energies are the same, and I feel the pain. Well, this pain in my hip went on for hours. I lied down on the couch in an effort to get comfortable, yet lying down seem to make it worse. Whether I stood, sat or was lying down, I was in horrible pain and discomfort. I kept trying to figure out what I had done to injure my hip.

Because I do not like to see in the spaces in-between I did not have the awareness of my spiritual sight, therefore it had not occurred to me that what I was feeling could be someone else, it's just not something that I like to think about if I can help it. I had learned many years ago that seeing the energies—the spaces in-between created many imbalances in my life, therefore as a natural protection I learned how to block out, or ignore what was right in front of my eyes. Its not as if I don't see the energies, I do, however it is much like when you are in a familiar space in your home—you know that the doorknobs and electrical outlets are there, yet unless you think about them or need to use them, it is as if they are not there. In fact, I think that even when we use the doorknobs everyday to open doors, we don't think about them at all, we simply use them to open the door not giving the knob a second thought, and this is how I have learned to live my physical life as normal as possible... I try not to give the spaces in-between a second thought.   I guess you could say that sometimes I have to deal with the "elephant in the room" - there are times when it is impossible to escape especially because of the empath energies. This was one such time. It is interesting because all at once it hit me like a ton of bricks, and I remember saying out loud *"ohhhhh, jeez, duh!"*... *"Where are you?"* Within a few moments I found the source of the pain in my hip. She was an older woman who had suffered from a broken hip before she died. Her story is quite the common one when it comes to the elderly. She fell and broke her hip, therefore it caused a chain of events that eventually lead to her death... *"unintended consequences"* is what she told me. She wore a red nightgown and her short grey hair was matted down on one side, I suppose her hair was that way because she had to lie on the hip that was not broke.   Anyway, when I did allow the communication, it was quite easy and took but a second. I told her *"look, your dead, but not dead, its time to go to heaven, through the light, you need to go home. And because I am an empath, or what some may call psychic, your being around me is causing me much pain in my hip"*. I told her that because I was plugged into her energy that my pain would not go away until she crossed over through the light to heaven. She was a little lady, of little words. Pretty much all she said was, *"Oh, okay"* and then she went home. I had learned that she loved daffodils and she wore a most beautiful perfume that smelled like a summer meadow of flowers. It was a most pleasant scent. She was earthbound because she did not know that she was dead. She was living her reality in the same manifestation as her life—her hip hurt, her hair was a mess, and she was still wearing her nightgown. It wasn't until I was able to connect with her and tell her that my hip hurt in the same way that her hip hurt that she woke from her earthbound state to an existence of the awareness that she had died. In essence she awoke from her dream state. Her name was Margaret.

The pain in my hip eased up quite a bit right after she made her transition. However, I still had a residue of the energies of her pain intertwined within my energies. I have learned that I have to treat my spiritual energy body much in the way I have to treat any other physical illness. I need medicine. The medicine I use to clear the earthbound energy injuries is God's love and light. I say a prayer and invoke the White Light of the Holy Spirit to cleanse my spiritual body and my physical space. I call in the angel's, masters and guides and ask them to please heal my energy body. I have learned the hard way that if I don't ask, they can't help. This is because if they stepped in and did it without my permission, they would in effect be robbing me of my free will – the only hard and fast rule of the universe is free will. If the angel's, masters and guides swooped in and saved the day without my permission or request they would be violating sacred law, and since they would never do that, I must ask.

Because I am an empath, it is necessary to fully cleanse my energies quite often because there are so many energies surrounding me all of the time. I find that taking a bath or shower is quite helpful and I also go outside in Mother Nature to drain off the residual earthbound energies. One thing that I have learned that is of upmost importance is that I must set my intent to heal and release all of the mixed energies from my energy body. If I am not willing to "let it go" it will remain with me until I do so. This is the power of the mind and soul that we all posses, once we understand that our thoughts and our intents do run the show of our life, life flows easier, and we stop being victims of pain and suffering. The mind is a powerful tool whether you are in the skin or not. It was the *thought* that the pain was real that made it real for Margaret. It wasn't until she changed her thoughts through my awareness that her reality changed. Truth be told, these are extremely hard feelings and emotions to live with while doing this work—helping the lost souls. I have had to learn how to try and detach myself from the lost soul's energies to a certain degree. What I do is I allow myself to feel what they are feeling while at the same time I keep the awareness in my mind that what I am physically feeling is not my pain, it is theirs. In other words, I do not allow myself to be pulled into their point of existence, because, when I do, and I am unaware, I wind up walking around for several hours feeling like I have a "broken hip" wondering what was wrong with me.

Many earthbounds unintentionally manifested the feeling of pain or depression thereby creating an illusion that the pain was indeed real. Logically, in the earthbounds mind the pain and their existence had to be real because they could *feel* the pain, and through their power of thought they were living in that manifestation. In the physical and spiritual realms, the pain is indeed real because thoughts of this pain do create a vibration. (*Oh, but if only people truly knew the power of their thoughts, they would indeed change them.*) We manifest our entire existence through our thoughts, whether we are in the physical or spirit realms. Thought manifestations are the reason why I can feel their pain, they are sending it out into the energies through vibrations that surround me in the spaces in-between.

One thing that I have learned in my life is that rarely do we embrace change. Whether it is good or bad has no relevance, it is still change. So, if the pain is gone and it has been a natural state of being for years a person does not feel like themselves, they somehow feel lost without it, and they do not feel normal without the pain. We could all learn a thing or two about the earthbound experience, the only thing that separates us from them is the skin. The pain of the heart and soul is a deep emotion and it can wreak havoc on the nervous system and our physical and spiritual bodies, it will never go away as long as we cling to it or think about it and own it as our identity. This is not unlike staying in an abusive relationship because of the fear of the unknown. Only, with these feelings we hang on to, in reality we are the abusers to ourselves, it is in these times when we must look into a mirror and admit: *"I did this, I am not a victim, and I can change"*.

Through this work in helping the lost souls I have to be the voice of reason…a grounding force by which they can hold on to. I guess you could say I work as a spiritual counselor, and I must find a way and the words to wake them to the realities of the abuse they are imposing upon themselves through their thought manifestations. When I speak to them, I tell them that we are here now, and I share with them the words I receive from spirit about their lives. It amazes them that I have information about them that *"no one could possible know"*. This validation allows them to think back to the past and remember the events of what actually happened, the words I speak to them about their lives creates a remembering to the events of their lives. Once the lost soul moves into the mindset of now, and of the present, they feel safe in going back to the experience that caused them to be in the earthbound state to begin with, and once they do this they can heal their pain. This acceptance is a major part of the healing process. It doesn't mean that the pain is absolved all of the way, it simply means that I have established a gateway by which they can open their hearts and mind to the other side, and once that happens they can make their transition home where they can receive further counseling and healing. During the process of communication, I would work hard to mask my own physical pain in an effort to lead them to the event that ended their lives. Many lost souls had the pain of loss or guilt that was holding them here on the earth. Oftentimes the connection to their earth family is strong and this connection of which I speak is through feelings. Many lost souls do not want to leave their families here on earth. I had to remain grounded within myself as not to take on what they were feeling. And when I felt serious pain I would try to keep it silent within myself because I felt that if I lost myself within their pain I would be stuck with them forever. I would try and tell them matter-of-factly what had caused their death, like: *"I feel as though your arm was broken, the back of my head feels as if I have been shot, my heart hurts...did you die of a heart attack?"* And so on.

Some of the lost soul work that I have done has been selfish on my part. I say this because much of the time it was not love in my heart to begin with that drove me to help them to make their transition to the other side. I wanted to remove them far and away from my energies, and I wanted to escape their pain and suffering which while they were in my presence I could feel. In my mind there was no better place than home... through the light into the loving arms of family and friends who were patiently awaiting their arrival.

Part 2

The Spark of the Divine

Chapter 5

The Migration

Friday August 25, 2006 was a beautiful day, and a typical afternoon for our family. We enjoyed our family dinner together and then around 5:00 pm David left the house to go to work for the night. Savannah and Luke were playing around the house and I was out on the back porch having a cup of coffee and a smoke. All of the sudden out of nowhere I started to feel off balanced, it was as if my body was sinking down into the earth and the earth felt as though it were tipping off its axis. Within minutes Savannah came to me with a worried look on her face. She told me that there were *a lot* of earthbounds in our home. I asked her how many, but she was a broken record and repeated what she had already told me and said with quite a bit of emotion *"there are a lot!"* That answer did not feel good to me, therefore I instructed her to go around the house and do a "head" count. Within several minutes she and Luke came back to me and told me that there were fifteen earthbound spirits in the house. I think my jaw must have hit the ground… it was shocking news to me!

Fifteen was not a number I ever wanted to hear in the same sentence with the words *earthbound spirits!*

Although we had helped quite a few lost souls within the last few weeks, this was a large number of souls to deal with all at the same time. Therefore, we were left speechless and stared at each other for a few minutes. I remember muttering silently *"I don't know what the hell is going on – this is too weird for me, and I have to find a way to make this stop."* Immediately, I called David and told him about the fifteen earthbound spirits. He told me that he did not know what to do. I told him that I was going to call Piper to see if she had any answers for me. The news baffled him... and I could feel that he was frustrated and confused. *I don't know what I thought he could do for me anyway, as he was driving a gas tanker down the road!* While I was talking to him on the phone, it got worse. I could feel more earthbound energy coming in around my body, and the spaces in-between were starting to get fuzzy with dark patches seemingly floating here and there. I told him I needed to get off the phone so I could call Piper right away.

I grabbed Savannah's hand and we went through every room in the house and counted a total of 54 earthbound spirits (*this count also included the earthbounds who were in our yard*). They had increased from 15 to 54 in about 30 minutes. Because I was so freaked out I reached for my phone and called David again. At this point he told me to call Piper, and maybe she could help us. Luke, Savannah and I were still speechless and staring at one another. The conversation went back and forth for a few minutes in an effort to try and figure out what was happening around us. For me, I was thinking or rather cursing, I could feel

Savannah plead to make it stop, and Luke was saying something like, "*this is so weird, this is strange*".

When I was able to bring myself back to my senses and snap out of the fog of shock, I quickly remembered the beautiful gift that Luke possessed. I asked him if he would ask grandpa why this was happening. We all agree this was a great idea, plus we were desperate to find answers. None of us wanted to deal with all of these dead people. Luke told me he would do the best he could and went into the house to find a quiet spot so he could carefully hear the messages from grandpa. Within a few minutes he came to me to tell me that grandpa had told him that we were about to experience something that is rare, yet it does and has happened to others who are like us. Luke informed me that grandpa said it was called a "*migration*" and that it would last about a week. He told me that we would have a lot of souls come through the house and that we should expect to see a rapid increase. Luke also said that grandpa told him that we could expect an increase of up to 150-200 that night-- (*and I thought that 50 was bad!*). Okay, now I was freaking out, and I had a hard time believing that this was happening to us.

Luke explained to us as best he could the information that grandpa had given to him. He told us that grandpa said that all was in perfect order, everything would be okay, and that we would know what to do. He also said that the weeks previous were a kind of initiation into what we were about to deal with on a larger scale of numbers. Well, that did make sense to me, because it was getting weirder and weirder each day as more earthbound spirits trickled into our home...I was starting to feel as if I were in the twilight-zone!

After the conversation with Luke I then knew it was imperative that I contact Piper. Immediately I called her. By the grace of God, Piper picked up the phone! I am sure that I sounded freaked out and I talked rather fast…I told her everything. She was very calm and collected. She told me right away that it was very important that we keep ourselves grounded. She instructed me to get some white candles and light them around the house. She said that the white candles were important and would help to keep the energy in our home clear and purified. She also said that it was important that we avoid eating anything with sugar, and that we should drink a lot of water. She advised me to place a tape recorder in the house, and to let it record, she told me that that we would receive messages on the tapes from spirit. I thanked her for taking time to help me and got off the phone because I knew I had a lot of work to do.

I took a look at the house around me and noticed that it was messy. Something within told me that we needed to get it cleaned up. I know that this sounds crazy, but I did not want all of the lost souls to be in a messy house…it was a respect thing. (*This goes back to my knowing that earthbound souls are people too!*) I am grateful that I followed that guidance because I know that moving our bodies and cleaning our home helped to keep us grounded, and centered. Also, cleaning the house burned excess anxiety out of our systems. After our house was cleaned we rushed over to Wal-Mart to get white candles, a tape recorder and cassette tapes. I was new to this crossing over thing and I did not know that I was supposed to have white candles, but it sure did feel right when Piper told me to do it. It was so weird because by the time we got to Wal-Mart we were surrounded by more earthbound spirits. We decided to tell grandpa and the angels to either take them to our house or have them wait in the car, because it was getting confusing trying to shop surrounded by a lot of earthbound people. We raced through the store and got our candles and tape recorder. I think I must have bought two dozen white candles.

It is difficult for me to try and explain what it was like for us that day. It was as though our souls kicked in to action, and we knew what we were doing, we were on a mission to send these lost souls home as soon as humanly possible… *and* what other options did we have? Talking to them and sending them to the light was the only way we knew how remove them from our space! After the initial shock wore off and we accepted that we had a job to do, if felt natural and familiar…something deep within us knew what we where supposed to do. We did not have any fear by this time. It became a matter of fact that we had a job to do. We came to the realization that we had been preparing for this moment in time over the last few weeks. It was all so surreal.

By the time we got home we were in a state of peace and calm, we were excited to get it done, yet we knew the seriousness. We had hundreds upon hundreds—yet even thousands of angels around us and they were creating an atmosphere of tranquility. They were the key to how we felt…the angels helped us tremendously!

We placed the candles all around our home, and I grabbed my notebook and the tape player and told the kids to meet me in the living room on the couch. As Luke was coming into the living room he told me *"Mom, there is a guy in our bathroom who died in the 9-11 terrorist attacks"*. This knowing really brought the seriousness of the situation into our hearts and minds. It was time to begin.

We sat down in the living room, and I hit the record button on the tape player. We all started talking at once trying to feel our way through the situation, then something happened that we did not expect—we started fighting and contradicting one-another. The energies quickly turned very uncomfortable. I became so frustrated that I went out to the back porch to have a smoke. Within a few moments Luke and Savannah joined me. They apologized for fighting, and I told them that it was okay because I felt the same way. It didn't take long before we were relaxed and calm again, and we realized that it felt much better outside. The energies were easier and it did not feel as if we were going to "blow-up". Because of this new awareness we all agreed that we would ask the angels to bring the earthbounds one by one out onto the back porch. We accepted that the energies in the house were too intense and mixed for our physical bodies. (*Through time we learned that water absorbs negative energies. This made perfect sense to us because our back porch faces a beautiful lake. I think the lake was the reason we could tolerate all of the energies of the lost souls… the lake and also the oak trees took in the energies.*) I decided to take the tape recorder into the house and sit it on the bar in the kitchen because I really did not want to carry it around with me. Also, I like to record events on paper, and I really did not know what the tape player would do for us as I had never experienced spirits on recording devices.

We started by doing individual crossings, talking with the earthbound soul one on one… so to speak, (*there were many beings helping us through this process*). We were a team, I call it the triangle—feel: me, hear: Luke, see: Savannah. I really don't think it would have been possible for us to have done what we did alone. We needed one-another so we could establish a solid communication with the lost souls.

Luke had a connection that was of a higher realm... he easily received advanced esoteric spiritual information through several means, his higher self (*connecting to The Divine Creator*), his spirit guides, and particularly grandpa. Luke was also a grounding force for me and Savannah in the way that he was so calm, and the words that he spoke to us through spirit had an effect that helped us to believe that all was well. This is a natural gift that Luke was born with—I call it "soothing energies". Savannah communicated by what she saw, and she was able to accurately describe the color of the lost soul's hair, their eyes, and what they were wearing. She also saw what she called splotches on the earthbounds body which was actually their physical injuries. There were times that she did see blood, and other horrific deformations of the injured soul. A unique thing that Savannah would do was to draw pictures of the lost souls as we talked to them. She is a little artist and has always loved to draw... particularly horses, which is her true love in this life. Anyway, she would draw a picture of the lost soul as we communicated with them. I think in a way that helped to keep her grounded and centered because it took her focus from her fear and calmed her nerves. Another beautiful gift that Savannah has is the fact that she can clearly see and speak to the angelic realms. This gift was a beautiful source of communication and information that helped the process of leading the lost soul home. I communicated through my gift of feel. During the process of communication I kept my eyes closed and allowed the energies to flow through, so that we could communicate with the earthbound people.

Together, through our gifts, we would bring the circumstances of the lost soul to light. It was interesting because the most contentious part of the process between the three of us was confirming the name of the lost soul. We discovered that the name of a person can be difficult in that they had had other lifetime names and also they have a name that they go by on the other side. Because our gifts are very different and we hear through different channels of communication, there were times that we would have 3 names for one lost soul. Needless to say, each time we worked our way to a consensus... even if it meant that I had to be the tie-breaker! In fact, there were several times as we were bickering with one-another the lost soul would crack up and start laughing. In fact, there were many times that we proved to be a wonderful source of entertainment for the lost souls. Through our experiences with the lost souls we learned that they were people too— with feelings, knowledge, and each one with a unique personality. I think this knowledge was an important aspect of our work. We talked to the lost souls in the same way we would communicate with any other person. We kept it real, which actually created an energy of belonging and comfort to the lost soul. It was always a simple communication. Not unlike if you were to meet a stranger on the street and have a casual conversation with them.

We had been at it for a while when Luke got up from his chair and looked through the French doors into our living room. He started laughing and told me that the other lost souls were talking to one-another and decided that they would form a line so they could talk to us on the back porch. That really touched my heart in a way that is hard to describe. These people needed our help, they were in a bad way, yet they were being respectful of our space and waiting patiently until we were done talking to the person who was in front of them. Luke said that grandpa told him that all of the lost souls who were in our presence were there purposefully. The angels, masters and guides "hand picked" the right match for us. The masterful workers of the spaces in-between have a knowing of all, they can see in all directions in time, and they know all of us to the core. So, I guess you could say they matched the earthbounds to us in a way that we would all be compatible, thereby creating a smoother experience.

We stayed out on the back porch for about an hour, and then we decided it was time for something to munch on—therefore we went into the house and raided the fridge. While we were at the dining room table snacking, Savannah started to laugh. She told me that the earthbound spirits were lined up at the tape recorder and taking turns talking into the microphone. This was so funny to us, because when I set the recorder on the bar earlier, I told all of the people in the room that if they wanted to, they could leave messages on the machine... *I had no idea they would actually do it.* We did all would could to help them feel as comfortable as possible, there were so many of them in our home I hoped that maybe the machine would entertain them for a bit. We also realized that they were all talking amongst themselves about *us.* They were telling each other that we were going to help them "go to heaven" I guess for some reason they had the perception that this was the norm... that this was the process of moving on. Who knows, it does seem logical that they were thinking that way, because as far as they knew this was the first time that they had been dead. They did not have any idea that the power of going home was really up to them.

The group of souls that we had on the first night was a mixture of several types of groups of people. The first "batch" was the ones who needed the one-on-one attention. These were the ones who would wait in line to be "served". Then there were the watchers—the observers. These were the ones who remained quiet and in the background of all the movement. Then there were the talkers, the ones who loved to talk on the recorder, these were the souls that also loved to talk to one another. We learned that some of the earthbounds had been with each other for quite some time. I think they must have found each other along their journeys of being earthbound. It is as simple as they met and then continued on their journey together. So, yes, earthbound people in their perception of their experiences do make friends, and stay together.

After a while we went back outside to our porch on the lake. The process by this time was flowing rather smoothly, and I think it was about 11:30pm so we had been at it for a couple of hours. We were talking to, and calling the lost souls out one-by-one… when one would make the transition, either Luke or Savannah would go to the door and open it and say *"next"* or *"its your turn to go to heaven"*… the most fascinating realization was the fact that many earthbound people do not like going through solid objects, even though they know that they can…it really freaks some of them out. I would say about 8 in 10 who were waiting at the door would not come outside with us until we opened the door for them. We found this to be quite common with most earthbound spirits. One of the times when Luke went to the door to let another earthbound out to the porch he paused for a minute looking inside the house and said *"oh, my gosh mom, they are inside talking with one-another and now they are crossing each other over!"* This news made us extremely happy, because we knew this would make our job a lot easier. Upon further inspection, he also noticed family members from the other side coming in to take the earthbound family member home with them. Savannah jumped up and looked through the glass doors and confirmed what Luke told us. She said the room was flashing with blinding lights all over the place. This was because when a soul crosses over there is a flash of white light in the energies. The angels, masters, and guides were working inside the house with the lost souls and because the lost souls had been around the house for several hours watching us do our work with other lost souls and witnessing others cross over, they were then able to make their transition without our aid. I told the kids that behavior was quite natural because no one wants to feel alone, and it is human nature to follow others. In times like this people like to have a feeling of belonging, and that others are experiencing what they are experiencing too. By this time everyone in the house knew that they were at a "*crossing over to heaven party*"... This was when we first discovered that we could do what we called "group crossings".

We made the decision to stay on the back porch and finish helping the lost souls who for some reason or another remained in line at the door. These were the ones who were the watchers. I think it was because they really needed reassurance from us that all was well, I think that they needed the personal human physical touch that we could offer them. This is another important aspect of the work that we do in helping lost souls home. Sometimes it is truly necessary that the message be delivered from someone that is in physical form and still in the body. It helps the lost soul to feel a little more real, and we would explain to them that we are still in our bodies, but that they are not, and I would tell them,"...*you're dead, but not dead!*". Savannah was also able to help a few of the lost souls in a very interesting way. She could slip right out of her body and take their hands, and help them through… she was in her spiritual body when she did this. Amazingly she did this quite naturally and effortlessly.

We did individual crossings Friday and Saturday, and we made a conscious effort to offer the personal attention to those in need of our reassurances. Sunday was the first day that we started to do the group crossings. During the group crossings the words that I spoke to the lost souls naturally flowed through my being. The messages that I conveyed to the group of souls were the words from a multitude of beings, such as messages from family members, who were in spirit and they would help me communicate by offering validations to the lost soul. I also received messages from spirit guides, the angels, and from my Higher Self that is connected to The Divine Creator. Fortunately, I always seemed to find the words that would touch the lost souls. I was being guided to say certain things, and so I said them, and it was different every time. As people were crossing over, Savannah said the flash of lights were blinding. For some reason I kept my eyes closed so that I could maintain my focus while I spoke to the earthbound group of people. Sunday through Wednesday we cleared out our living room and den, and went back and forth from one room to the other for several hours each day. We were getting a lot of help from the angels and spirits from the other side. Although there were quite a bit of mixed energies in our home, the angels, masters and guides seemed to maintain a healthy balance in the energies creating a situation whereby we could function in our physical bodies. These heavenly helpers kept us grounded, and it felt as though we had loving arms around us and shielding us at all times. Savannah and Luke told me that a huge gold angel stood behind me, and when times got really tough, she grew huge. They said her feet were as big as my body. They told me that she was big naturally, however, when I would get scared—she got bigger. It was kind of funny because the earthbounds started calling me *"the lady with the big angel"*. I am not sure if she was for me or, for them, or for all of us. I have since come to learn that this "big angel" is indeed one of my guardian angels. Her name is Seriliah… most of the time I call her "big mamma".

Several days after the migration was over, grandpa told Luke that the angels, masters and guides had been planning the migration for some time, and that they had been gathering up and collecting the lost souls for two years preparing for this event *(our earth years- time for them is all the same)*. Grandpa said that they were all very happy and call it a huge success, and they were pleased to tell us that we helped all of the lost souls that had been guided to our home.

The Spark of The Divine

Through my experiences with the lost souls, I have found that love is the key. In my communication with them I let them know that God loves them no matter what they have done and that their work here on earth has been completed and that it is time for them to go home where they are loved and wanted. Something interesting happens to me when they understand the messages that I deliver to them from spirit. *As soon as they feel and remember Mother-Father Gods love, I see a tiny white spark. Isn't that interesting?*

Further discovery has led me to understand the following:

The spark of The Divine is the *key* to making the transition to the other side. When I see the spark, I know that the person is about to make the transition through the light, I know that at that moment...within a single instant, a remembering has taken place within the soul. The spark of The Divine is an awareness of the soul—it is the sudden realization of whence the soul came. The spark is the truth and the light which is the love of our Heavenly Mother-Father God, whom is The Divine Creator, and of Jesus and of the Masters and of *ALL* of creation. This Divine light is the light that can heal any and all situations and this light, put simply, is *PURE LOVE* in its totality... and this light, which is pure love...this light, is what makes everything real. The spark of The Divine resides in all forms of life...this includes plants, trees, animals and all living creatures. The spark is love and this is the pure love of God Whom created all. This spark is Gods creation...*it is God.* Therefore, anything that is not of love and light is a delusion and of the earth plane and of our earthly manifestations.

We are all energy and light in our natural state of being. Therefore, if we focus on negative and darkness we carry the energy of the earth and the low level feelings of depression and earthly matters, which in effect shrouds the light that is naturally housed within all. And because of these low level feelings of depression, fear, anger and so on, the souls who were coming through our home had lost their way. They had lost the will to remember who they were and were living an existence based on delusions.

We could learn a thing or two from the earthbound experience. When we become prisoners of the earthly realm we do forget about the light that is within, through free will, we simply forget. The light is still within all, it is merely muted, seemingly dimmer by lower energies such as fear, hate and anger. The key to ignite the spark, and light the within is to remember from whence we came, and to remember that all is love. *This process is as natural as breathing.*

Unfortunately, it becomes second nature whilst in our physical bodies to build up a defense system and worry about all of the possible things that can happen to us. We come into this earth and live with pain and suffering and in many ways the pain and suffering defines who we are and this is often carried over into death. The energy of that physical pain remains manifest in our spirit and our soul. All of our beliefs and feelings do not simply fade just because we are no longer in our physical bodies—no indeed…this low energy is carried over in fullness into our death experience. When a person chooses to live in a miserable existence they then become that misery energy. They become the energy of the depression and the energy of hate. These low level energies can literally flood the human flesh that manifests into the soul and spirit. This is seemingly a complex and contradictory statement in that I believe that our souls are perfect and will always be. However, this energy, the negative energy is a strong force. It is the contrast experience to the energy of love. This contrast of feelings and emotions are the basic reason that we come upon this earth to experience. *However, it is also the truth that the mission that we come here to complete, is that of remembering who we are and where we came from.*

When I reach out to a lost soul who is one with the low level physical energies, I have to do a lot of convincing to this person that they are indeed very much loved. This is the key to helping a person transition to the otherside. Everyone wants to believe that someone loves them. In fact, this is the greatest tragedy of the human race, many do not believe that they are loved, and they feel as though they are not worthy of unconditional love—the love of The Divine Creator. This is interesting to me, especially in the realms of the religious sects. Often, I have found that guilt plays a huge part in a soul rejecting the love that is necessary to accept in order for them to make the transition home to heaven. The religious guilt that is pushed upon them and received by them throughout their physical lifetime make it almost impossible for them to feel that they are a loving child of God, and a precious person who is loved. Therefore, the many examples of Christ's life and his *unconditional* love did not seep into their consciousness. Unfortunately, within the physical realms there is more power given to the fear of hell-fire, wrongdoing and damnation. There is a purpose to our life here on this planet as physical beings and it is to experience in all shapes and forms the low level energy, because one can not get this experience in our natural state of being on the otherside. It is through the experiences of the contrast that we all grow and expand our spirit. These struggles and then triumphs are the necessary path to spiritual growth. *These are the words that I share with the lost souls... these are the words that often offer that remembering of who they are in truth.*

I talk to the lost souls and explain to them that they simply have come to this earth to experience and that we are here to complete certain soul tasks which we chose before we came here. This is where people seem to get hung up. They judge their mistakes harshly and then they are upset that they made these so called "sins". And because they've make these mistakes, they fear the hand of God and they are ashamed of what they have done, thereby, making it difficult for them to feel the love and light of God—because of this, they close their hearts off from the source of all that is love and they live in a fog of denial. Therefore, because of free will they can create their own reality that is full of shame and self deprecation. They no longer feel as though they belong to the higher realms, in other words, often they feel as they do not deserve a place in heaven. I speak the word heaven because the souls that the angels bring to me...*they all know this word... Heaven is a universal word.* Heaven is a key word of sorts... the soul has a remembering of the energies of this word. When the lost soul opens their heart to this remembering they are easily convinced to receive this love which they are desperately in need of. This needn't take long because love is a powerful tool in helping people—this is the only way I have found to reach the lost soul...through love.

There have been many times when I have been too tired and ornery to help some of the lost souls who have crossed my path. When this happens to me, I have learned that I can borrow the energy and endless supply of love from the angels, masters, and guides. The ingredient of love is essential to have whilst trying to reach the lost souls—one must dig deep beyond the dark and lonely energy that is causing them to forget that they are of The Divine, and that they are creations of God. It is extremely difficult for many of the souls to realize that God is loving and patient. It is only when the soul looks within and realizes that they did this to themselves—because in truth, nothing is really ever done without our free will…only then can they move on, they can then realize that they are not a victim. I know that I may sound like a broken record, yet, in all situations, love is the instant and constant cure to all. When we realize this, everything else falls away and there is no longer the energy of hate and despair.

When you look upon anyone on this earth and if you look with your heart, you will see the spark of The Divine within all. It does not matter what atrocities they may have committed in this lifetime or the wrongs of which you think they have done, pure and simple, they are just as much a child of God as you are. Take off the judgment cap and send out the love from your heart. With the spark of The Divine, miracles of love are inevitable.

One thing that I must mention in this chapter is this: *EVERYONE can always go home!* There is nothing true about a soul going home prematurely. This would make God an idiot, and since we know that this not the case, and to our core we all hold the belief of truth, which is: *ALL is in Divine order!* The truth is, when a person is ready to make the transition, the light appears. The lost soul must evolve to a readiness…a remembering in order for their light to appear. Henceforth, there is never unbalance between this world and the otherside. Yes, it is true that many times when a soul crosses over, they are still in distress and are in need of counseling. Therefore, the healing is the first stop for the lost soul. There are people on the other side who are waiting to greet the soul to take them to the proper place for counseling and healing. Everyone is always expected when they arrive because all is known on the otherside and everything is synchronistic and orchestrated. All are aware and all are prepared to help each and everyone. There are many souls, beings and angels in place to help each and every creation whom makes the transition home to heaven. *There is no such thing as a premature crossing,* because there has to be awareness within ones soul, a remembering—this is the spark of The Divine and it happens every single time an earthbound spirit reaches the awareness of who they are and where they came from. The spark of The Divine is in essence the love of God and is the creation of all things. All things that have been created find their origin in the spark of The Divine.

Each spark of The Divine is as different in the same way each snowflake is different....There are no two sparks that are the same!

The pages that follow are full of the stories of some of the lost souls that we experienced before, during and after the migration. During this period this of time, I went through tremendous ups and downs and doubts and fears. I learned that the road less traveled was to be a difficult path to follow. Although I had made the changes and thought that I had accepted my spiritual gifts...I soon discovered that this period of time in my life would be one of the most challenging experiences, it was indeed a test of will to know myself. Through this journey, I learned to practice faith with the knowing that everything would be alright. I learned the valuable lesson that stability of the mind was of most importance. I prayed to Mother-Father God and connected to the beauty of The Divine. I wrote my feelings and experiences in a journal, and I documented the events as they happened. I connected with the angels, and did a lot of meditating. However, there were times where I refused to allow the information to flow smoothly, therefore, in those times I would become blocked, and stuck. Then there were times when I flowed with spirit and allowed me to be me. I was up and down for two years straight, and the thought crossed my mind a million times: *"I am gonna be me, its okay to be who I am, just keep going, have faith!"* and at the end of the day I would have a deep spiritual understanding of my mission and purpose. Deep down I knew that no matter what people would say or think—it really did not matter. It was how I felt about myself that really determined whether or not I believed in all of the strange and curious events of my life. Acceptance comes in little tiny ripples of belief. I learned that it took one step at a time to allow my natural state of being to flow. Therefore, in the spirit of flow, within the pages that follow, I tell the story of our experiences with the many lost souls.

Part 3

The Lost Souls

.

Chapter 6

Earthbound Dreams, Lifetimes at Night

Earthbound dreams happen to a person who is sensitive to the energies. Another word for sensitive in my vocabulary is *"empath"*. When one is an empath, they are extremely sensitive to the energies of the spaces in-between. Earthbound dreams happen to empaths more often than they realize. If I go to sleep and an earthbound spirit is in my space oftentimes I will have a dream whereby the earthbound spirit is a visitor. Within many of these dreams I have experienced the message of how the lost soul died. The event is replayed in my dream, and often it is as if I am a third party watching the events unfold of the last minute of the person's physical life. I have also had earthbound dreams whereby I have total communication with the lost soul. Most often when the dream comes in this form, they are asking me why things are the way they are in their life. These dream experiences come with the territory of the gifts that I possess.

Throughout my life, I have always had what I classified as nightmares. I would wake up drenched in sweat and exhausted from the events of the dreams. I have come to the realization that many of these dreams that I have had throughout my life were indeed earthbound dreams. These are the dreams that I call *"crazy ass dreams"*. This is how I have decided to classify them because usually when I wake up from an earthbound dream the first thing that goes through my mind is *"Whoa! That was a crazy ass dream!"* When I have these dreams, I wake in a state of disarray, whereby I am ornery and cussing because of the experience. These dreams seem to happen to me when there is an earthbound within or around my physical space at the time I go to sleep. Somehow they are able to slip into my dream state and become one with my mind and I become one with their existence. Sometimes I experience these dreams as an on-looker, other times I experience these dreams as part of the cast of characters in the dream, and then other times somehow I become the earthbound and experience what they are experiencing.

Regardless of the part that I play in these dreams, they are always highly emotional dreams filled with messages from the lost soul—most of the time the dreams pertain to their physical life, or physical death. There are times when they take me to their home, they show me their home in its manifestation of when they were living, and then they will show me their home in its present day condition. If they have the awareness that the home is not the same, they want to know why everything has changed. Either way, they have the energy of a confused soul.

Throughout many of these dreams I am many places on the time-line—I am whipped around in time, taken here and there quite rapidly. I have been taken to parties, I have been taken to weddings, and I have been taken to just about every experience and place the earthbound wants to show me from their lifetime.

The earthbound will use symbols, persons, places or things in an effort to communicate with me about their issues, questions or problems.

These dreams are like no other as they are full of the real emotion connected to the lifetime of the lost soul. The colors and the events are real, yet surreal at the same time. They are unlike the dreams that I experience when I sleep at night and go to the otherside…these are the pleasant heavenly dreams, the dreams of which I communicate with the angels, masters and guides. Earthbound dreams are somewhat unlike prophetic dreams that I have that speak to the future. However, the future or prophetic dreams are more like the earthbound dreams than the heavenly ones. Differentiating between the different types of dreams is quite easy. Here is one of my prophetic dreams from my journal:

"I have what I call crazy ass dreams some nights when I go to sleep. It just dawned on me however, that one of the dreams I had recently, has actually happened.

I had a dream that I was in a building with a lot of people and a guy came in with a gun and just as a matter of fact started shooting people. He was calm and he just systematically reloaded and continued to shoot whoever was standing.

Over the last few weeks, a song has been going through my head, the one from John Denver. Take me home, West Virginia.... Well yesterday, there was a shooting at Virginia Tech. It was described by the witnesses almost exactly as it was in my dream. Incidentally, in the song take me home, I knew it related to someone dying".

The earthbound dreams are with people who seem unfamiliar, yet somehow I know a whole lot about them. The earthbound dreams seem to come with distinct and vibrant colors, yet it has a muted and foggy feel about it, and the energies have the air of confusion, not so unlike the prophetic dreams. However, the dreams of the future almost seem as though I am looking at them on a page, somehow experiencing these events from a story of a book and they always leave me feeling as if something is about to come to pass. They are as profound as the earthbound dreams and I have experienced *"lifetimes at night"* when all three of these dream states have merged together, and the experience proved to be quite surreal.

When I awake from earthbound dreams, I wake with a start and a feeling of dread. These feelings will not go away as long as the earthbound that was with me in my dream is still with me in the physical, therefore, it is always in my best interest to have a conversation with the lost soul and tell them that it is time to go home to heaven. I realize now that these dreams are a valuable tool which can be used in assisting and helping these lost souls to the otherside. When the lost soul shows me everything about themselves that they can remember, and they put their life in my memory along with the feelings they have—I have a deep understanding of how they feel, and why they are earthbound. This knowing gives me the tools in order to help the lost soul make the transition.

Before I came to the realization that what I was experiencing was earthbound dreams, I was left with the feelings of depression for days and the event or dream would continue to haunt my existence. I did not have the understanding as I do now that what I was experiencing was communication from a lost soul— I thought that I was prone to crazy nightmares, and there was nothing that I could do about it and I felt victimized all of the time by my dreams. I never liked to watch horror movies because they were often like the dreams, which would lead me to wonder what was wrong with me...which at the time also feed into my victim state of mind.

One thing that most earthbound spirits have in common is that they truly feel victimized. They are angry, sad, depressed and scared. They feel alone in their pain and feel emotional hurt on a deep level. So many times as we are living our lives we have a hard time moving past certain events that have caused us much pain. Many of us who have suffered through traumatic events often replay these events in our minds over and over again—sometimes to the point that we must seek counseling and maybe even use medications for awhile because these events have changed the chemicals in our brains. This is no different for earthbound spirits. Many of them are caught up in the event or multiple events of their life and they keep playing them over and over again. On some level the earthbound spirits are much like those of us "in the skin" when it comes to dealing with traumatic emotions, except theirs is a much lonelier existence and they can't seem to get any help for their problems as they keep "living" or replaying the events over an over again.

Who are they to seek for counseling? Some earthbound spirits do talk with one another because they have a realization that they are in the same existence, much like when we go to the grocery store we have an awareness and talk to the people around us. However, this communication does not help to elevate them to the level of healing because they are now in a state where low level emotions and feelings rule their worlds. Much in the same way, if you are an alcoholic, and you don't want to drink… you really should not go into bars. Other earthbound spirits are not capable to help, because if they were, they would not be in the earthbound state themselves.

There are also times when lost souls will hitchhike through my dreams. They are simply players and are much like background characters to the story that my soul or mind is playing out. This type of dream can be quite amusing to me in that I realize during the dream that some of the people in my dream are earthbound spirits. It is akin to someone who is putting on a play for an audience, and then all of the sudden several of the audience members decide that they want to be in the play. Well, the people performing and putting on the play don't want to cause a scene because they have a huge audience. It can be quite shocking that someone would have the nerve to invade upon the stage, therefore the actor's adlib and continue on with the play. After a short while these invaders become a part of the play and the unknowing audience believes that these people are a part of the play while all along the actors had to readjust so the play can move foreword, un-interrupted. This analogy is much like when earthbounds hitchhike into my dreams. I know that they are there, but I go on with my dream state. These are the dreams that I know are for me, they are about me, not about earthbound spirits. They are not *crazy ass dreams* because the topics of the dreams aren't telling the story of the earthbound spirit. These dreams are telling me a story for my life and sending me messages to help me on my life path.

I do however have one type of dream that lost souls can never enter, *unless* my soul is taking them to the light during my dream state. These are the heavenly otherside dreams. If I allow them into my dream, I simply help them through the light to heaven, I do not see them again when I wake up. I call these dreams soul travel, and I have an awareness that these dreams are a part of my work as a guardian.

The Floating Guy

This was one of the stranger earthbound dreams that I have experience thus far. This guy kept showing me the same thing over and over again. The first thing that he showed me was work shoes that were black and they were in the hallway by my front door, and then he showed me a cigarette butt that caught on fire. After the cigarette butt, he took me to my screened-in porch. Then the strangest thing happened—his eye popped out and he floated towards the floor. He was caught up in a thought loop and at times he would become his earthbound self that was in the now. The shoes in the hallway were woman's dress shoes, and he was trying to show me that his wife was still alive. Therefore, he simply showed me her work shoes. He kept showing me himself floating down to the ground slowly, it was eerie because he only had the top half of his body, he was see through and his left eye kept popping out as he descended to the ground leaving his eye suspended in the air for a few moments and then it would slowly float down to the ground following his body, he showed me this loop several times.

He knew that he was dead, but he wasn't sure if I knew that he was dead, so this was how he was showing me. It was creepy and eerie, yet, not unnerving to me because of that fact that I have seen these visions and events so often throughout my life. Don't get me wrong because there is always that initial shock to what I see, but then something within me just chalks it up to another lesson of awareness and knowing that came my way... *regarding my spiritual gifts, I have come to a place of acceptance.*

He used my home and my surroundings to communicate with me... he was too afraid to take me to the actual place of his murder.

His name was Edward Frank (first and middle) but often people called him Ed. He was eyewitness to an event that could put someone away in jail for a long time. He was murdered, but before he died he was brutally attacked, they poked out his eyes, and pushed him over some sort of ledge where he fell to his death. I think the reason they destroyed his eyes was because if he survived the fall, they did not want him to identify anyone in a police line-up. The reason he showed me the flaming cigarette was because it was the last event that he saw with his physical eyes...he saw someone lighting and smoking a cigarette before his eyes were gouged out. I believe the reason he kept taking me to my back porch was because he was pushed over a bridge into a body of water, a river. This is relevant to the symbolism of his communication, as my screened-in porch overlooks a lake. I think his wife's name is Marjorie. He came to me with the full awareness that he was no longer in the physical realms... in other words; he knew that he had been murdered. It was important to him that he communicated with someone who was in the physical, and his message to me was: *"I was murdered because of this case!"* He also said that he loved his wife dearly...he said *"I am so sorry honey!" I'm okay now!* He made his transition to the other side when I talked to him after I woke-up.

I chose to tell his story first because often this is what it is like experiencing earthbound dreams. Some of these dreams seem to start out like a mystery novel. The mystery is in the clues that they show me and sometimes it is very cryptic because they have a hard time remembering really what happened to them, it truly is much like a suspense novel...or a detective story.

An Old Man with Alzheimer's, a Cop and a Security Guard

This earthbound dream had three earthbound spirits telling me their story all at once. It was a mixed-up and confusing dream... being here, there, and everywhere at once. This is much like if you are in a room and everyone is trying to talk to you all at once!

In the beginning of this dream I saw an old man walking down the sidewalk with his little dog. It was so funny because this man had a dog that looked just like him. He was in his seventies and I could see that he had carrot red hair albeit full of grey, as to show his age, at this point in his life it looked to be a pale pale orange and his dog was a little red hairy thing who was aged as well. It was interesting because through the facial features he looked so much like his dog. The dog was a cocker spaniel. I knew at once that he had Alzheimer's and that he was not supposed to be wandering around walking his dog. When I connected to his energies all of the sudden I felt lost, and then I went somewhere else, the scene totally changed, and my belongings were gone and replaced by other things. *This is a representation of what happens to them when they lose track of earth time.*

I went to a counter to ask the people in the building where my things were and they told me they did not know—(*this was me being him in the dream*). Then a cop came up to me and told me that he had received a complaint about my dogs barking and that he had the authority to arrest me, and he was a real jerk. Because I was a bit out of sorts, I thought that he was talking about my dogs that I had years ago, and no longer had, so I told him that I did not have the dogs any longer. He told me to wait, and then he disappeared. When he walked away I was no longer in a confused state, as the old man was nowhere to be seen... he had disappeared. Then a lady dressed in a security outfit started telling me that my dogs were getting on her nerves. She told me that she was the one who reported me to the cop. She described my back yard and told me that she knew that I had the barking foursome. I gathered that she was taking up residence as an earthbound spirit in the house across the lake. She told me that her father was sick and that the constant barking was annoying them. I asked her if she would give me a few days to correct the situation, and she agreed, although the cop would not hear of it.

This is the sort of earthbound dream that can get very confusing, and it wasn't until I woke that I was able to get my wits about me. I gathered the lost souls...the cop, the security guard, and the old man, and told them that it was time for them to go home to heaven... They crossed over immediately. I had no interest in trying to learn about the who's and why's regarding this earthbound dream, I simply told them to go home.

Sometimes it is not necessary to learn the circumstances of the death, or about the life and death of the lost soul. This is because it is not necessary for them to make the transition. I do not need the tool of communication or information in order for them to go through the light. Sometimes the lost soul only needs to hear this phrase: *"You're dead, but not dead... go through the light, its heaven!"* When they hear that...they go home!

Oftentimes the lost souls use events or people in my life to validate to me that they have been around me and in my personal space. They make a real effort to show me that they indeed know about my life, this is their way of validating to me that they are really in my life.

In their earthbound state they are experiencing a split reality of sorts they are here and they are there. As an example, the security guard lady thought that she was still home taking care of her father while at the same time she was at my house and my barking dogs were getting on her nerves. It is like a play and it is so weird how they continue their roles they had in life, thus, it carries over to their earthbound state, such as the cop who still thought he was a cop and had the authority to arrest me. He did not know that he was dead, therefore his life was business as usual and he was going around in the earthbound plane policing and arresting other earthbounds. Somehow I get sucked into the unreality and find myself actually feeling what they feel, therefore, I go along with whatever is happening, like when I begged the security guard lady to give me three days to fix the barking problem and she said fine, but the cop who was a hard ass, told me that it was unacceptable. Earthbound spirits become immersed in the lives of their living counterparts while at the same time they are in the same existence of what they were doing when they died. They merge the two together which I think makes it all the more confusing for them, but they go along with the unreality anyway.

The Construction Site Brawl

This was a dream that I will not forget anytime soon because my earthbound spirit showed me his death, the full event. Dreams like these are the reason why I do not like to watch tv shows about solving murders, because I experience these horrific events in a unique way, up close and personal, and I know that these crazy murders *really do happen!*.

This earthbound wanted me to know that he was at my house so he showed me a vision whereby he was very angry with me for ignoring him over the previous days. Because he was angry, he started to throw my lawn furniture into the lake. He immediately grabbed my attention because of his violent behavior. During these dreams I have the awareness that they are earthbound dreams, however, there is also a part of me that becomes immersed in the events creating a situation whereby it feels very real— just like it is happening to me and I am experiencing it. He was frustrated and angry at me because I was ignoring him and he could not get my attention. I had been spending many hours out on my back porch writing this book and ignoring those of the spaces in-between who had passed through my sphere of existence. While I was writing my book I did not want to do any of the lost soul work. It created within me the energy that I so much wanted to be without, so as to make a clear and concise record of what has happened to me I did not want other energies to bleed through into the writing process. At any rate, I did ignore this guy and kept my shields up keeping him out of my house and porch. Therefore he was left to try and get my attention in my back yard and I simply ignored him. I have learned that the earthbound spirit does not need to be standing right next to my bed to slip into my dreams. I have discovered they could be in my yard or even in my neighbor's house, and all they have to do is set their intent and bingo, they are in. Therefore, from my back yard he decided to tell me his story.

After he got my attention by throwing all of my lawn furniture into the lake he took me to a construction site where a construction crew of about five men was building a house. The house was at the stage of where the foundation was complete and the two by fours were constructed as to build the walls. I could see all the way through the house to the otherside of the construction site, so it was at the early stages of fabrication. All of the sudden a huge fight broke out between the construction crew... and it became violent and viscous, they were rolling around, punching, kicking, and throwing things at one-another. Things went really bad when one of the guys grabbed a big drill, threw another man down to the ground and held him down as he drilled a hole into his forehead. It made a loud creepy drilling sound as the guy lay screaming in agony...the screamer was the guy who was the earthbound in my dream. His name was Sam.

I woke with a major jolt, and it took me a minute to gather my thoughts... the images and sounds were still streaming through my consciousness. I talked to Sam and told him that he needed to move on, it was time to go home, and that all would be okay. He made his transition within minutes. I am not sure why I had to see this event. Although, I do think I was needed to calm him down as he was still furious and angry...just as he was when he was fighting at the construction site. Once he realized that his anger was keeping him stuck, he released it and moved on to the other side.

The Lost Daughter...A Soul in Stasis

She showed me her house where she grew up, and she showed me the before and the now. She also showed me a wallet with pictures of her family and her dear father who looked a lot like the actor John Ritter. Within her wallet she found her home address. She traveled to her home alone, and then once she got to the familiar surroundings it started to jog her memories, but then she realized that it had changed and then she became confused. She was extremely close with her father during her lifetime and she was in a panic to find him. She had been in an earthbound slumber for many years and when she woke-up, she tried to go back home only to find that everything had changed.

When she made contact with me, she immediately took me to her home. Her home was in California somewhere on the coast and it was a beach house. She showed me the pool in the back yard, she was quite upset that it had not been cared for and the pool was empty. She took me to a party that had been thrown for her while she was living...it was her graduation party, I saw her father and her friends at this party... it was all so real!

She had been a kidnap victim of rape and murder. Fortunately, her family was able to lay her to rest as she had been found. Because she had died such a violent death when she was killed, she was jolted into a shock, and her complete shock put her soul in what is called *stasis*. It is like a stand still in time, until the soul can heal enough to awaken. Upon awakening the soul can then figure out what had happened. She had been in a soul stasis for about 30 earth years.

I believe her father helped to orchestrate her finding me through the help of the angels. Her father had died since her death, and he helped watch over her soul while she was in stasis. This does happen often, the angels and masters work together and match lost souls with people like me. They know who can work with whom. They know who to bring to me so I can help them make the transition to the otherside. During my earthbound dream, although she took me to her home, she never took me to the place and time of her death. I think some sort of healing took place while she was in stasis so she did not have to re-live the event of her death over and over again.

While a soul is in stasis it is surrounded in Gods strong and loving arms and is protected from harm. Stasis is a healing period for the soul. The soul is in a coma state without any awareness of anything. It is as simple as falling asleep at night and then waking up the next morning. The soul is also surrounded at all times in a strong healing bubble of sorts, there seems to be a place somewhere out there in the universe that is set aside for these poor lost wounded souls. Their soul is guarded the entire time by the person's guardian angels, spirit guides and family members. Visiting of the soul in stasis is extremely limited. It is a very delicate state for the soul; therefore, it is guarded by the power of God.

She was brought to me because I looked a lot like a good friend of hers that she loved and trusted, therefore, she was comfortable talking with me and asking me for my help. In fact, at first she thought I was her friend, and I don't remember if I even told her while she was showing me her story that I was not her friend. I think I just played along with it because I was in a dream state as well.

After she took me around on the little field trip I was able to talk to her, I listened to her and when I woke up from the dream we continued the conversation. I asked her father to come in, and he did. I told her that he would be able to explain all that had happened and that it was time for her to go home with him through the light. She started to cry when she saw him, she turned her head to face me and with tears in her eyes she thanked me for helping her, then she made her transition. I took a deep breath of relief as she disappeared.

These dreams that have heartwarming conclusions always leave me in the state of contemplation of all the things that happened to the poor soul and yet in the so called end, with everything wrapped up, I am left with the distinct feeling that all had been the way it should have been, it was the way it was planned to be. That is a big thought to try and explain…it is just what it is—the feeling that all is complete and is as it should be, including my brief journey through her life. Her name was Suzan.

God and the angels do know all things and they are masterful in carrying out plans to help the lost souls, they are creative in the most infinitesimal way. Each and every event is carefully planned out to assure success. God and the angels do have the ultimate power—however; they will never usurp our free will. Therefore, they have to plan around the fact that we might not do these things that are for our own good. I know that this knowing feels complicated in that God knows all things…I call it organized chaos. There is always the element of planning and preparedness and a working together in concert on the otherside to help these things come to pass. This is because of our free will, and they have to work around the free will element.

When we talk about the mind it is important to remember that even dreams are real to our life, they become a part of who we are regardless if they are "real", or "not real" as they do become a part of who we are. There is something that happens to us when we wake from these dreams…we are relieved that they were *just a dream*. However, that relief is also a sign that on a certain level we thought the events of the dream were real. Therefore, the essence or energies of what we experienced in these dream states are somewhat carried over into our minds and life. It is perfectly understandable to try and erase and tell ourselves that these things that happen to us while our heads are on the pillow were not real, however, they do affect our lives in a vast way. There are many lessons within our dreams, and through my experiences, I have learned much from the earthbound dreams—the *lifetimes at night*.

Soul Stasis

The definition of stasis according to Encarta dictionary is; *a state in which there is neither motion nor development, often resulting from opposing forces balancing each other.*

When something horrific happens to a person the event puts too much fear and dark emotion into the soul all at once. Therefore, everything must come to a complete stop as to balance the scales. Hence, God and the angels and healers put in and around the soul strong and precise healing energy to balance the opposing forces or energies. Until the energies are balanced the soul remains in stasis.

There are several types of soul stasis. A soul can be in a form of stasis while the person is still living and functioning on the earth in the physical body. It often happens to people who are in a state of PTSD. When a person seems to be out of their mind, and doing things totally uncharacteristic, or seen as crazy... this is often the case while the soul is in a stasis healing. This healing process is necessary because the mission and the lifetime of the soul are not complete, and because the person took on too much negative or traumatic energy... it creates an imbalance that is dangerous (*in a way*) to the soul. This is more about life purpose, and completing life purpose. If something happens to someone that put the soul off path significantly, it can cause eternal imbalance. In this case, the soul is part unaware, part of the soul is somewhere in the universe that is set aside for this type of healing... the soul is sitting, or lying while sleeping and surrounded by powerful healers and angels who work to balance the energies in and around the soul.

Another form of stasis occurs to people who have experienced horrific, shocking or traumatic events. Because the event is unbearable to remember, they block it from their memory. This is why they do not remember huge blocks of time. The block is actually a form of stasis healing, whereby healing is taking place over the event. It is only when the person is ready for the event to be remembered, that it can come to the mind of the person. The person can then safely heal the memory. This is a form of Gods protection and love. *Again, I think it has to do with life purpose and keeping balance in all things.* Personally, I know this because it has happened to me. I have experienced this type of soul stasis. I lost a huge block of time, although it is hard to explain because I was there, but I was not there.... I have a remembering of vague things...as if they are dreams. Another form of soul stasis is when a person is in shock.

Chapter 7

My Lady, Missing, but not Lost...

7/7/2007

As I laid my head down on my pillow to sleep that night I settled into my cozy mattress and took a deep breath. Then it came...the energy around me became deep—it was a darkness that crept into my soul and reminded me of my spiritual gifts that at this moment I was thinking of more as a curse. Please angels! I pleaded in a whisper. Please Archangel Michael, take this soul away. I am too tired and I want to sleep. I promise I will take care of her another time. I was searching my mind when I would possibly be willingly take this energy back on, deep down I knew I was in denial, that I was bluffing and had no intention or at least not anytime in the near future for asking for her energy—nope, not anytime soon. Besides, I consoled myself...It was the end of a day that had been busy, and I was tired.

Many times this had happened to me, and often I would become belligerent, the angels and masters knew my temperament well. However, it never seemed to alter their loving and calm countenance. I would always feel their understanding and patience... their whisperings and songs to my heart sang of love and understanding. They always seemed to have a one track mind—they diligently reminded me through guidance and a gentle nudging towards my path and of my life purpose that I was here to complete. They would speak to my soul—*"little one this is your path, you are safe, you are loved."* In my mind I would always acknowledge that they had a deeper understanding and knew of my soul's plan, however, it never seemed to stop my late night tantrums. I was like a two year old that could not see the bigger picture. I would cry and whine hoping that I could get my way. I would go to bed angry, frustrated and wondering if I would ever get a break from all of this, only to awaken the next morning with a deep understanding of the job I was to do. Then I would feel guilty, I knew that these souls were lost and they only needed a few moments of my time. However, these few moments were adding up, hence, adding to my frustrations. My soul would travel the universe throughout the night, gathering up lost souls and bring them to my home so that I could cross them over in my waking moments. There were times that I would cross them over as my body lay sleeping. This was the rollercoaster of my life. I felt as though I was experiencing whiplash. It was difficult to make the transition from calming serenity leading to my night's sleep, to the sudden surge of earthbound energy wafting about my bed and consciousness.

As her energy surrounded my body, I drifted off to sleep—I simply chose to ignore her as I closed my eyes mumbling to myself, *"what the hell happened to free will"*... *"This is my bed in my home and I am going to sleep"..."fine,"* I said to her *"hover over me all night, I don't care"* and with that, I turned my body and faced the other direction away from her and drifted off to sleep as the energy of pins and needles stabbed into my body.

In the past, this sort of thing would send me into a panic. However, my recent knowledge and education into the spiritual realms had given me a great weapon to my state of mind. Now that I knew what this was, I knew that I was not in any harm, so I would simply choose to live with the uncomfortable physical feelings that I would receive from the earthbound energies. I could get so hardheaded and stubborn at times, so much so that I would choose to live with the pain instead of helping the person cross over. This would be my way of standing my ground. *"Uh, hello...I have FREE WILL, remember!"* I would cry out to the angels and masters.

During the earthbound dreams there is awareness, it is twofold—I am aware of my body in slumber as my soul watches the visions before me.

Her energy permeated my body and soul, and even before she took me there, I felt it, I knew it. I knew what was about to happen and I did not want to go there, I did not want to see this, I did not want to experience this. I pleaded to her with every fiber of my being..."*no, no, I don't want to go there...I do not want to see this, please just let me be!*" I had a deep understanding to my core of the horrors I was about to witness, and I knew instinctively that I did not want her to take me there. As I pulled back from her energy I was released, everything went black, it was almost as if I were in a state of unconsciousness...yet the awareness of the self was still there.

Seconds later I was taken to the place of her last breath, and I knew that what I was about to witness was going to send sheer terror into my being. I had been to this place of horror before as I was not a newcomer to earthbound dreams. I had seen many horrible events and traumas unfold before my eyes.

However, I felt this one to be different...yes, this one was personal. This one was going to get inside my heart and soul, and I knew it was going to be hard to watch without detached emotions. To the depths of my being I sensed that I was about to be drawn into a real life horror movie.

I looked around me into the darkness desperately trying to gather a sense of where I was—I knew that this was a desolate place. I smelled the rich damp earth beneath my feet. I was surrounded by trees, and I knew that I was somewhere in a forest. My mind and eyes immediately zoomed into the spot. This was what she had brought me here to see. I saw the freshly dug hole in the earth...I knew it at once...this was to be a grave...her grave.

Once again I fought back, I was trying to escape and everything went black. Coming back I saw her, she was standing with her back to me on the edge of the hole in the ground. The only thing separating our bodies was the fresh dug grave. I saw her body in its fullness—she was wearing very short blue jean shorts that hugged her slim hips. Her red t-shirt was tight fitting with cap sleeves. My eyes followed the line of her body that seemed to stand still with time. Her straight hair met her shoulder blades in a straight cut line. Her hair was the color of mahogany, deep brown with beautiful auburn. Her hair was not red, nor was it brown. She had a delicate frame—she was slender and tall, her height reaching about 5'7".

She fell into the hole as if she were pushed from the front, once again I blacked out from the vision only to be brought back within seconds to the dark woods. This time when I came back, the assault on her body was in progress. I stood at the edge of the hole in the ground watching helplessly as her attackers viscously abused her body. She was putting up a fight and all I could do was stand by and watch it happen. I was in a place in time that I knew full well had already happened, as real as the event felt, I knew that I was a silent observer to past events leading to her last breaths…I could do nothing to save her. The feelings of rage and horror coursed through my being and the anger overtook my soul and sleeping body.

There were two attackers one was a Hispanic female she was wearing black pants and a white t-shirt. She was not tall in structure; her height was approximately 5'2". She had a curvy womanly figure, she was not thin nor was she fat. Her hair was a dark chocolate brown and it fell upon her shoulders, it had a wave to it, it looked as though she had curled it with hot rollers. She had much control over the situation and I felt that she was the one who was the mastermind behind this brutal attack. She put her heart and soul into mutilating and humiliating my lady. Her counterpart was a male Hispanic, it is hard for me to remember much about him as I felt he was simply along for the ride, he was following instructions from his female mate. He was the same height as my lady reaching about 5'7" with dark brown hair that was nearly black in color. He was wearing dark pants and a button up work shirt. The two attackers worked in unison never giving my lady a chance to escape. I have thought long and hard whether or not to put the race of the perpetrators into this book, as I do not want to disparage anyone or want anyone to think that I am attacking a race of people. I am simply the messenger of this story and this is how it happened, these are the people I saw.

My lady was precise in what she wanted me to see. As she tried to fight her way out of the hole that was about five feet deep I saw her bloodied muddy face. I watched as they mutilated her and raped her body. They beat her horribly while they took turns raping and attacking her. Her head pounded up against the wall of dirt as they violated her body, she wanted me to see her face—and I did.

I will never forget her face.

She had bangs that framed her heart shaped face. She had fair skin that I knew could easily burn in the sun. I could see her eyebrows and they were nicely shaped yet thin, I remember thinking they must have been professionally done. Her eyes were a hazel color with specks of green. Although her lips were not full, the bottom lip was slightly fuller than the top. Her nose was straight and fit her face perfectly. Even through the blood and mud I could see that she was a very pretty young woman, it was hard to tell her age but I thought she could not be older than twenty-three. This time when I blacked out it was because I was too traumatized to witness anymore. I had seen the look in her eyes—it was that of acceptance, a knowing that these were the last few moments of her life—and she knew it. *I had witnessed her last look.*

When I came back, the first that thing she showed me was a grave that had been covered over, and at that moment I had a knowing that she was not their first victim, there were two other graves next to hers. She continued showing me specific things. She showed me the leaves on the ground by and on her grave—they were the color of autumn. She was trying to give me a timestamp as to when her attack took place. I was still trying to understand why she needed me to know all of these details concerning her death. I knew this was a premeditated murder, but I was confused with the feeling that she was picked at random. My confusion was laid to rest by the last scene of this earthbound dream. I learned at that time that there was one particular item for which she had been chosen. This was the part of the dream that was personal. This was the part that shook me to my knees, and my soul suddenly vibrated with deep sorrow and grief. This was last vision she showed me.

As I looked around into the darkness I saw a white blanket lying on the ground. The contrast of the white color on the dark earth drew me to the item next to the grave—it had been placed at the foot of her grave. The Hispanic woman bent over and unfolded the blanket, revealing to my eyes that within the blanket lay a small baby who was about 3 months old. I crumbled within, and my soul ached with the knowledge that this event was a kidnapping. *"They killed my lady and stole her baby!"* were the sounds that echoed within my heart, the sounds repeated within me many times, and I cried out within *"who does these things...how could humans be so selfish, brutal and viscous?"* Then a fear took hold of me and I wondered what was to become of this innocent child. Consequently, my fears became a panic. My lady was precise in what she showed me about her baby. She wanted me to know that the baby was male, so she showed me a vision of his penis and I also noticed that he had been circumcised. The next thing I saw was the Hispanic woman lying down on the ground next to her husband. I now had a knowing—they were more than just partners in crime, they were married. The woman placed the baby boy in-between the two of them. She then patted the ground where my lady lay deep within the earth in the slumber of death, as she patted the earth she said *"there, there, now everything is going to be okay."* This was an emotional nightmare. Could it be possible that these two people felt that they were deserving of this child, one who was not rightfully theirs?   The woman who had just murdered my lady seemed to beam at the child as if she had just given birth to him. She cradled him within her arms and lovingly looked at him as if he were her own.

My lady had completed her mission and I was free from the earthbound dream.   My body woke with a jolt and I was covered in sweat, my hair was soaking wet.   I was frozen in my bed and did not move for quite some time, as I was trying to hold myself together. I remember thinking that I was not going to cry, because if I did start crying, I might not be able to stop. I knew that I was in shock. The panic for the child was palpable and I had a tremendous fear of what was to become of him. I knew that the murderers believed in a sick and twisted way that he belonged to them. They felt that they earned the right to have him, *it was sickening*.   In their minds he belonged to them, he was now their child. I could not stop thinking about what they were capable of doing, things that I knew they would do if they became angry or psychotic again. What of the times when the woman became stressed out, what if the baby boy started crying because he missed his mother? Would they start hitting him, would he be next? The questions started coming into my mind at lightening speed and my mind was drowning within them. I had to stop thinking about it to save my sanity.

I muddled through the day with awareness that my lady was still very close to me, I felt her desperation. She wanted and needed my help. I did not know what to do as I was not a crime fighter, besides I had no idea where to start looking for clues. I just wanted this situation to go away, my fight mode had left and I was in the flight mode. Finally, she convinced me to look on the internet for missing people. I knew that this was a bad idea as

I was not in the state of mind after the night before to deal with more missing people and some of the terrible things that happened to them. Something happens to me when I look at the pictures and photos—I start getting horrendous visions of what happened to some of the missing people. I looked through several websites but, after a few moments I closed the computer. I told her I was sorry but that I was not strong enough to do this now. I told her if she cared anything about me she would make her transition to heaven through the light, I asked her to do it for me. I told her that as long as she stayed in this state she would carry with her the energy of the attack and her desperate fear for her child. In turn, I would be made to suffer through it with her as I was an empath, and her energy was intertwined with mine. The immediate solution to this problem for the both of us was for her to make her transition to the other side. I explained to her that she could come back in a healthier state, and then I could and would help her. She refused to make the transition. She wanted me to document what I had seen. She wanted me to write her story.

Reluctantly I opened my computer, but the fear overtook me and I quickly shut it. I was in deep dark fear and panic. I did not want to write this story because then it would mean that I would have to re-live the event. Once was enough for me. I could not endure the pain of the horrible events again, it was too soon. It was still to close to me and I knew that I had to be gentle with myself. After a few moments of going back and forth with each other, I relented. She was determined and I knew that she was not going to stop asking until I fulfilled her request. I had my motives in that I was willing to do anything I could to escape her energy. I knew that she needed to move on. I was afraid that if she did not go now, she would become earthbound for many years to come. She needed to make the transition immediately. So I did what I do, *anything it takes to get them through the light*.

I wrote her story as detached as possible—I recorded the facts of the event. It was as if I were a news reporter relaying the tragic event without emotion. Towards the end of documenting the story I started to become weak in spirit, and body and I knew that I had had all I could take. I had no more to give her. Out of my desperation, I called Luke and Savannah into my bedroom. I told them that I needed their help in crossing someone over. The look on their faces told me that they could feel the energy and they knew this was an urgent situation. I told them not to inquire as to what had happened to her. I promised them it was something that they did not need, nor want to know. I told them an abbreviated version. I deliberately left out the gruesome details of the story while silently asking God and the angels to shield their minds from the events of my ladies death.

We did what we do…we talked with her, we consoled her. We explained that everything would be alright and that she had many people waiting for her on the otherside. We asked her to trust us—we told her that we loved her and that she could come back and act as a guardian angel to her child. We explained to her that he was going to need her help and that while she was in the earthbound state, she would be doing harm to him. We explained that he was connected to her through the energies and that he needed pure loving energy wrapped around him, not the energy of the last few moments of her life. After a few moments of talking she grasped the understanding of what we were trying to relay. We saw the spark of The Divine, and then she slowly made her transition. Within seconds she came back and thanked us for all of the help that we had given her. She was still in a delicate state and left quickly. We learned that she was in counseling on the otherside and that many others were there to help her make her transition. I was relieved to hear that she was on her way to remembering that she was an eternal being of The Divine. She now knew that everything was going to be okay. Her soul was now wrapped in loving divine peace. My lady was missing to those of the earth, but she was no longer a lost soul. *She was now home.* When I woke from the dream, I knew her name for a few seconds but then for some reason I blocked it from my memory, so I simply called her my lady. Once I became more emotionally ready, I remembered her name. However, in telling her story I kept "*my lady*" as her name. Her name was Katherine.

I was an emotional wreck the days that followed her transition. I was consumed with anger and fear, and I wanted more than anything to hunt the murderers down and snatch the baby from them. Finally, after a few days of mourning I reached out to Piper. I needed to talk to someone who had experienced what I had. I left a frantic message on her machine telling her about a vision that I had concerning a missing baby. Within a few hours she returned my call, I was upset and she calmed me down and told me to talk through it. I told her about my earthbound dream, and explained all of the events that happened with my lady including her transition. Piper told me that the key was when I wrote it down, my lady needed to know that she would not be forgotten. She needed to know that someone heard her story. I was so intertwined in the story that it did not even dawn on me how important it was to record the events for my lady. I told Piper that I was distraught over the fact that they were still in possession of the child. I held back the tears as I had been doing for days, and now the lump in my throat the size of an orange. My body ached for the child, and mourned for my lady. Piper told me about a similar situation that happened to her years ago and that she understood how extremely difficult it was to live with this knowledge. I told her that these people were sick—they actually thought this was their baby. They were going on with their lives as if nothing out of the ordinary had happened. In their minds...they were a happy family.

As I took her through the vision I began to realize that Piper was with me psychically in the place of my ladies death, I felt as if she were seeing the visions right along with me. It gave me great solace to have someone to talk to that could see as I could. I knew that she felt how fearful I was for the child, so she offered me some words of deep ancient wisdom. These are words that are not easily swallowed, but when in the grasp of these understandings the knowledge of the universe is opened before our eyes.

She told me of the child and his choice to come upon this earth into this situation. She explained to me that he knew full well of the circumstances he was coming into on this earth. Once again she told me this was of his choosing. She told me that she knew my lady was not their only victim and that he chose to come into this life deliberately to help them and in doing so he would help others. She knew that because of him they were no longer going to engage in this murderous activity. Having him in their lives would change them for the better. He opened their hearts to unconditional love. As she spoke I interrupted her, I started to understand what she was trying to reveal to me and said, *"Do you mean that he is the light in the dark"*. I could see her loving smile as she told me *"right...that is exactly right."* She offered gently reassurances that all was the way it was supposed to be. I told her that I had a fear for my safety if I were to reveal the story. I felt that danger would come my way if I were to stir the pot...she concurred and told me this situation would work out naturally through the hands of the universe. She told me that she had experienced a situation in her life that she was going to speak up, but an angel came before her, stood right in front of her and warned her to stay out of the situation. He told her that her life would be in danger if she pursued any further, thus she stopped. She told me that there was a reason that I felt cautious and this was for my own protection.

Even though I understood that my lady was a sacrificial lamb of sorts and that her child would be changing the course of many people's lives, I was still in a place of fear for him. Knowing this, Piper took me forward in time of the life of the child. I saw the little boy playing—he had beautiful light brown hair with adorable curls that bounced as he ran around the room. *I saw him*—he was playing in a living room with toys and running around and happy. He appeared just as a normal toddler...it was as if nothing traumatic in his life had ever taken place. He had on a diaper and a white t-shirt, and I saw his dimpled elbows. For the first time a smile crossed my face for the child. The energy surrounding him was peaceful and happy. This was what I needed—I needed the reassurance that he was going to be safe from harm. *He was the light in the dark.*

Chapter 8

I'm Dead...?

Many of the lost souls who have crossed my path have no idea that they are dead. They simply are unaware of that fact, and it is my job and duty to reveal this to them. I have been met with many different types of reactions. The most common reaction is that of absolute shock and surprise. Once the initial shock wears off, I can start the communication process. These are the souls who hear from me *"you're dead, but not dead!"*...

Robin Hood?!

One afternoon as I walked into the den Savannah said: *"Mom there is a guy standing in the kitchen dressed up like Robin Hood"*. David had just walked into the room behind me. The thought crossed my mind that now we had totally lost it. *Now we are seeing Robin Hood!* My first response was to laugh out loud. I think I even said out loud *"What the hell is going on around here!"* The thought was quickly removed as Luke informed us that in fact the character of Robin Hood could be easily explained. His name was Ty, and he had died in an automobile accident Halloween of 2005. He had gone to a party dressed as Robin Hood. He drank until he was drunk. Unfortunately, he decided to get behind the wheel of a car and drive intoxicated. We learned that he was a young man of 22 years. He had dark brown hair and was a quiet fellow; it was interesting because in his earthbound state, he was still intoxicated.

We learned early on that when the lost souls came to us they did so in the manifestation of their experience when they died. This explained why Ty was still in his Halloween costume and drunk. As it had been for us for several days, he was not alone. At this point they seemed to come to us in groups of two. There was another man named Frank who was with him, yet they were not connected in the same death, nor did they know each other in life… they were simply there standing in our kitchen…together. Frank made his transition to the otherside quite quickly, and because Ty listened to us as we explained that they were dead but not dead, and it was time to go home through the light—he left shortly after Frank.

We found it quite comical in many instances that it was a *"follow the leader"* experience with so many of the lost souls that came our way. We learned also that the angels did *"hand-pick"* the souls that they would bring to our home. They always knew what would happen. Therefore, Frank was brought along with Ty because the angels knew that Ty would not make his transition if it were not for witnessing Frank crossing over. To this day, I get a good laugh whenever I think of our *"Robin Hood"* experience!

<u>Scantily Dressed!</u>

Earlier on the same day of our *"Robin Hood"* experience, I was out on the front porch grouting our new tile that David had laid just days before. It was a hot August afternoon; therefore I wore as little as possible. I was wearing shorts and a summer top that was low cut, tight and held up by spaghetti string straps. Savannah came out to the porch and told me that she needed my help with a guy who had just come into the house. He was making her feel uncomfortable because all she could hear was a *"creepy breathing sound"* that scared her. It took us a few minutes to figure this one out, because he was wearing the oddest outfit that we had seen to date... or so we thought, keeping in mind that later that day we saw *"Robin Hood"*.

He was wearing leather chaps and a cowboy vest over a light colored shirt. He was wearing what appeared to be cowboy boots, and an odd looking cowboy hat. The thing that kind of caught us off guard and caused us to scratch our heads was that he was wearing a scarf in the shape of a triangle over his nose and mouth. Quite frankly, he looked like a bank robber to us, which seemed likely though odd because he was wearing a gun belt with two guns hanging on both of his hips. It was like he stepped out of an old western cowboys and Indians show.

Further inquiry lead us to the fact that he had died many many years earlier. He told us that he was the one who took the wagon of supplies into towns for people way back when in the western states, through the *"Wild West"*. He was the supply wagon. We learned that back then, it was horse and buggy, not an 18 wheeler! He told us that everyone carried guns, because it was not safe on the trail otherwise. He told us also that it would often take week's in-between settlements or towns. One afternoon he was traveling through a rough trail one of the horses lost its footing, and it created a chain reaction with his wagon, eventually he basically had a wagon wreck. Because he was in the middle of nowhere, and at that time there was no such thing as cell phones, or "*the next exit*" off the freeway, he actually died of dehydration. He was injured in his accident, and he ran out of his food and water supply. He tried to make it with his horse and then by foot after the horse had expired—he simply could not.

We found out that the reason he had the bandana over his mouth was to keep from breathing the dust, I guess you could say he traveled a dusty trail. His name was Vincent. He was in his thirties or early forties. He was never married, nor did he have any children. Although he had been in an earthbound state for years, he was still experiencing all of his physical emotions before he died. He was very thirsty and had a hard time breathing, thus the "*creepy breathing sounds*" that Savannah heard.

When he followed Savannah out to the porch, I was not in the mood to stop what I was doing because I was trying to get the grout in the tile. I was dripping with sweat, and I continued with my work as I informed him that it was time for him to go home to heaven... I offered my regular spill, of "*hey, look mister, you're dead, but not dead!*"

He listened to me intently for a minute, and then he blurted out as he was looking down my top, "*why ma'am, you are scantily dressed!*" and just about that time he glanced over his shoulder and noticed two teenage girls walking down the street in very short pants, he could not believe how little the women were wearing. I told him he had no business looking down my top anyway! I literally laughed out loud when he made his comments about how little I wore. I told him that he should realize that he had been dead for a very long time and that a lot had changed since he was alive. I also told him that his breathing and thirst problem would go away as soon as he went home to heaven. He hung around for a few more minutes before he made his transition. I haven't seen or heard from him since. I think he must have been glad to be home, as some of the lost souls do come back in spirit and say thank you... he never did! To this day, when I think about Vincent I have a good laugh. Poor fellow...he had no idea that he was dead!

She Fainted!

This is one of those stories that happened during the migration that was surprising and also very funny! This event happened during one of our group crossings. We really enjoyed doing this work with groups of people because it was always so easy. We would answer the questions of one person and the others who were present and listening inevitably found that they had similar questions so we did not have to answer the same question over and over again.

One of the most popular questions was *"Where are we going, and what is in the light?"* This particular time I felt the strong love and presence of Jesus so my answer to them was: *"Jesus loves you and is waiting for you on the otherside through the light"*. One of the ladies in our group fell flat on her face, she fainted! She was so excited to know that she was going to see Jesus that in her manifestation, she stopped breathing and passed out! I know that it doesn't make logical sense because she was in spirit and without her body that was in need of oxygen. I think this experience brings home the understanding that our minds and thoughts are very powerful and that they do control our state of being, whether we be in the physical or spiritual body... in other words, our thoughts rule the universe.

So obviously, she did not think of herself as dead. She was an older lady who loved her church and her bible, Jesus was the love of her life. Meeting him was akin to a young girl meeting a rock star or Elvis. Of course, we immediately went to her and helped her up from the ground. She did not waste anytime making her transition to the otherside once she came too.

It was an exiting time for all of the lost souls who were present in the room because the energy that permeated from our *"fainted lady"* was pure love and happiness, and everyone present at the time could feel the beauty coming from her being. All of the lost souls that were in the room made a smooth transition with smiles and chuckles. This experience left me, Luke and Savannah laughing for quite a while. And to this day whenever I think of her, I can't help but to laugh and smile, and I feel her loving energies. She was a beautiful person and is a beautiful soul full of love, joy and happiness. *For some reason...we never did get her name.*

Earthbound Shopping

One day late in the afternoon some time after the migration I was in my bedroom watching tv and Luke and Savannah were in the den watching tv as well. All of the sudden, my tv switched over to a shopping channel. I grabbed my remote wondering if I had accidentally touched it and had changed the channel unknowingly. The remote was placed next to me on my bed, so I grabbed it and switched the channel back to what I was watching. A few seconds later my tv switched back to the same shopping channel. This went on for a few minutes... The channel kept changing back and forth and I was certain that I was not doing it but the tv kept going back to the shopping channel. By this time I started to hear Luke and Savannah from the den saying things like: *"Hey! Did you do that! Quit changing the channel!"*

I went into the den and told them that my tv kept going back to the shopping channel and they told me that it was happening to them as well. After a few minutes we realized that maybe it was someone else doing this. Therefore, we decided to find the culprit. I found her in my bedroom watching the shopping channel. We figured out why this was happening, it was because when she was alive, she loved to watch the shopping channel on tv, and since she did not know that she was dead, she continued on with her life as usual... watching the shopping channel.

It was through her power of thought that created the manifestation of the shopping channel on our tv, in other words, it was through the energies that she was able to control our tv's. We learned that she died of a heart attack while she was sitting in her chair in front of her tv watching the shopping channel. She was quite addicted to watching these shows, and even after we told her that she was dead, but not dead... she did not want to leave because she feared that she would not be able to watch her shows from heaven. It was only until we told her that she could do anything she wanted to do when she went to heaven...

including watching her shows that helped her come to a realization that she could indeed go home.

Another tool that I used to convince her to go home was the fact that since I was plugged into her energies and I am and empath I would feel like I was having a heart attack until she crossed over. It was through this communication coupled with the fact that she could watch tv in heaven that she agreed to go home. Also, when I spoke of her chest pain, it brought her into the now... as she could feel it too. I told her that the pain in her chest would go away for the both of us once she went through the light. I do laugh when I think about her, or whenever I visit the shopping channel—I think of her and giggle!

One Life for Another

Vivian missed the animal on the road saving the animals life, but then she lost control of her car and crashed...she died from injuries of the accident. She was a woman in her mid sixties and had already retired, however she became a realtor because she loved life, loved people, and loved to work. On the day of her death she was on her way to show a house.

We learned that she had breast cancer, however that did not stop her, she kept on working and loving life. I thought it to be quite a beautiful ending to her life that she died of a car accident in an effort to save a wild animals life, instead of through the cancer that was in her body. She was so cute as she held on to her "*pocket book*" and looked quite proper and queen like, her hair and clothes were in order, and well thought out. I could tell that she lived an orderly and organized life, and that people loved to be in her presence because she was such a joy to be with at all times.

She was smooth energy…even as an earthbound spirit. She simply did not know that she was dead. I love to think about her in that her last thoughts were of compassion and love towards one of Gods beautiful creatures. I believe that now she is working as a guardian angel for many beings on this earth, and that she, even now brings the energy of joy and happiness to all. I do believe that she was an angel incarnate…in other words, she is an angelic being who chose to incarnate into the physical in order to bring about the energies of love and balance into the many lives that she touched while she walked this earth…*including mine.*

I Can't Breath!

During the migration as per Pipers suggestion we did record the events of those nights on tape. On the first night while we were out on the back porch crossing individuals over we became tired and hungry and decided that it was a good time to take a break. On the way into the house Savannah and I both commented on the fact that we were having a difficult time breathing, and that we needed to find who ever it was that couldn't breath so that we could cross them over. As we walked into the house towards the dining room it became increasingly difficult to breath.

Once we were in the dining room I thought it would be a good time to check and see if we had any messages on the tape recorder. I turned the tape off and I rewound it for a few seconds.

When I turned it back on we could hear a lady saying that she could not breathe. Savannah blurted out, *"That was scary!"* Then Luke said, *"Oh my we should have had her come out earlier!"* After I told the lady that we just needed to cross her over, she gasped and said..."*I didn't know!*" Luke told us that she had died in a fire and she still thought that she was in her home trying to get out. In her earthbound state she was still experiencing the last few moments of her death over and over again. Immediately we took her out to the back porch and told her that everything would be alright, and that it was time for her to go to heaven. She came out of her fog of confusion within a few minutes of our conversation and made her transition to the other side.

She lived alone in her home with her cat, which also died in the fire. She was a teacher, and well liked in her community. She was around 50 years old, and I believe her name was Frances.

I felt bad for her as she had no idea that she had died, and for several earth years she had been experiencing the time loop of the last few minutes of her life whereby she was down on the floor of her living room trying desperately to make it to the front door. Her home was full of smoke making it nearly impossible to breathe. I am sorry to say that when she was discovered by the rescue team, they found her body in her living room just inches from her front door.

Chapter 9

Mischievous Souls

If you remember anything at all that is written in this book please remember this:

A *jackass on any plane is still the same!*

As a sensitive I have encountered mischievous earthbounds who will try to upset me by sending me negative emotions and feelings just for spite. These lost souls were mean when they were still alive in their bodies, and they were people who liked causing mischief and trouble. It seems as though it was their purpose to get attention and they are the ones who are often trying to get a reaction from people.

These mischievous souls are now in a state where most people cannot see them. Therefore, they are being ignored, and because of this they act out and create certain behaviors in order to get the attention they feel that they need. Thus, they have learned to be quite effective and are masterful in scaring unsuspecting people. Most of all they are usually quite angry because they are still in a place where they want to take it out on everyone who is around them.

Remembering that they can not physically harm you is important. They can however affect the energy around you thereby creating an energy that is similar to what can happen to us whilst in the physical. For example, if your friend is in a bad mood... somehow after a while you too are in a bad mood.

The only thing that the earthbound spirit can do to you is to make you *feel* as if they can harm you, however they cannot, nor can they ever possess your body. This is a matter of natural law, in that two things can not occupy one space at the same time. This natural law applies to our physical bodies. Your soul is your soul and can never be taken over by anyone or anything. You are the master of your mind, body and soul. God and the angels are the keepers of your soul. Therefore, it is helpful to remember that you are always protected.

There is something that has caused quite a bit of confusion through time regarding these mischievous souls... and that is that fact that people think that they can do harm to those of us on the physical plane. The confusion lies within the fact that we are all energy beings of light... this being said, everyone can feel the energies. Therefore, if there is a lost soul who is in your presence who died in a fire, and you are an empath, it may very well feel as if the earthbound spirit is choking you because you can not breathe. The simple fact is, if you feel this way, you are plugging into the energies of the lost soul, and you are experiencing what the lost soul is feeling, and this is possible because you are feeling it through the energies. I give many great examples about energy transference throughout this book, particularly in chapter 4 titled: *Do You Feel What I Feel.*

Free will rules the universe, therefore if you want to believe that you can be taken over, then that will be your experience. It is simply up to you and your perceptions of your life. In dealing with this mischievous bunch of lost souls it is important to remember that your mind is a most powerful tool. This knowledge will keep you grounded and centered, therefore keep that in mind if you start to freak-out. Use your mind to your advantage by staying calm and in your own personal power if you are ever in the presence of a pissed off lost soul. Another thing that is valuable to remember is that whenever you are feeling weak of body, mind, soul and spirit; ask for help from the angels. You can always ask them to bring the energy of calm to your physical mind and body. Simply ask God and the angels to take your fears. Then you can release your fears and accept the healing energy that comes to you.

One might ask the question as to how a person became a mischievous soul. The answer is as simple as; whatever the person experienced in their life, it simply carries over to the death experience. Some examples are: Rebellious teenagers painting graffiti, people who become involved with gangs and violence, high strung people with road rage...the truck driver sitting in the diner grabbing the waitresses' ass....you know, mischievous! People who are not happy unless they are miserable, people who like to fight, people who like to be angry at someone all of the time, alcoholics, drug addicts… this list could go on and on, yet I think you get the picture. Any emotion that is of low level energy that brings harm to anyone can create this type of earthbound manifestation.

One night as I about to doze off to sleep in my bed, I was jolted out of my pre-slumber by a mischievous soul. She got right into my face and said in a most fierce way: *"I know who you are!"* and then she spit. She was trying to intimidate me. It was interesting because she had heard from other earthbounds that I had been helping some of the lost soul's home to heaven. Apparently, she did not like that some of her friends, through me, made the transition—seemingly leaving her behind. I have to admit that for a split second it worked and she did scare the crap out of me because she came from out of nowhere. Plus, she had the element of surprise on me because I was half-awake.

She was about 5'6 and had jet black hair which had been dyed to be that color – She was around 16 or 17 years old. She was your typical super rebellious teen who was going through her "black clothes" stage when she died. Her rebellion did carry over into her death experience, and she was, I am sure, any parent's nightmare. I could just picture her mom saying something like, *"Where did my pretty little girl go?"* I did what I do, and I did tell her that she was dead and that it was time to go to the light, however, she was not accepting of the message. Therefore, I did have her removed from my space. I sent her far and away from my place of abode. After she left, I worked hard in conjunction with the angels to remove her energies from my energies. I have learned since, that she has made her transition through the help of another guardian like me. I think the angels allowed her into my space because I was at a point in my growth where I was learning how to set boundaries and limits when it came to dealing with the lost souls. I had to learn how to say no. And in this case, I did. Her name was Alicia.

Metaphorically speaking, when you go into this battle you must be equipped, and prepared. I don't really like using the word battle when it comes to this work, however in the case of mischievous souls it can be quite the test of will. Surround your body with a protective shield and this is the white light of Gods love, The Holy Spirit or whatever you chose to call it, just surround your body, home and any place you want with the white light. Call upon Archangel Michael and the band of mercy. He is the angel who can effectively clear the energy using his fiery sword and he is always ready and willing to serve. Use the ascended masters and spirit guides and call in countless numbers of angels. Everyone is willing ready and grateful to help the lost soul...most importantly *mischievous* souls! These heavenly helpers are in place to help the lost souls and those who are here to help them, you know, people like me. Heavenly helpers always answer the call to help. They never forsake anyone.

The warrior spirit and the fire in the belly are needed when confronted with these troubled and oftentimes belligerent souls. Our emotions are given to us from God for a reason. Every part of our being was created deliberately. We are to use our gifts whether we think of them as bad or good. And in the work of the soul we are given tools to fight what are sometimes fierce battles. These are the battles of the will and energies. I have found that it is a good thing that I have the gift of gab. I keep talking to the lost soul while tuning into the energies—this seems to buy me some time and eventually they start listening to what I am trying to tell them. I do not filter any of the messages that come through for them because it is always the thing that I think would be stupid to say that creates the spark and touches them and reaches them. So, this battle is fought with love and courage and a lot of talking.

The angels keep it pretty still for me regarding things moving around my house because I hate it when objects start moving around so I have made a point to tell the angels that is something they need to control. They keep the lost souls contained, or with their feet on the ground, so to speak. I try to keep in mind that the battle that I am fighting is for the good of the lost soul. I am fighting their personal demons which are keeping them in the earthbound state. I feel that it is important to understand that these earthbound souls do affect the vibration of the earth and all who exist here. Their low energies can create uncomfortable feelings that one cannot explain—these are the energies of the souls who are on such a low vibration they create a thickness in the air that mutes out the light of the Holy Spirit.

There was a lost soul who I helped who literally thought he was the spawn of Satan. He had lived what many would consider an evil life. My purpose in helping him was to show him that he was a creation of The Divine just as all of us are. Because of the terrible deeds that he had done throughout his life he became his own judge and jury, casting himself as a demon or devil. Through his thoughts about himself he created this manifestation. His face was blood red and his lips were black. He looked like what many would consider a demon. But, I think he was tired because when he was brought to me, he had already surrendered. Or, maybe he had just accepted the fact that he was a bad person so he was no longer fighting the internal battle of guilt and shame, and his negative energies had dwindled quite a bit. He sparked and went home through the light with his guardian angels. No biggie. I get so much help from heavenly helpers and I really don't have to do much except say a few words because they do the bulk of the work. I am grateful to Mother-Father God and I have more faith than I ever thought was possible because of the fact that I know I am not alone whilst I do this work.

Then there are the times that I have to fight fire with fire. I have learned to bless the part of my life that was dark, I was born into a situation whereby I was a latchkey kid, my mom worked and my dad was gone. Therefore, at a very young age I learned the realities of life. I learned how to survive the "evils" of the world, and my perception was that the world was not a very friendly place to be. Therefore, there is a part of me that was born out of some very tough times when I was a young child. This is the part of me that I have to pull out and bring to the showdown with the mischievous soul. This work is not always a day in Sunday school. Sometimes I have to fight on their level to get through to them. I have learned that I have to stand in my power, and not budge. I look them straight in the eyes, and I don't blink. When I plug into a lost soul that I know doesn't have a problem with curse words I treat them the same as I would any other person who is treating me horribly and trying to scare me...I cuss right back. The story of the rebellious and ornery teenager is one such case.

The Rebellious and Ornery Teenager

One afternoon after David had gone to work, I was in the living room watching tv and Luke and Savannah were in the den watching some kids shows. All of the sudden I heard a banging noise coming from the direction of my bedroom. My thoughts did a few twists and turns trying to figure out the source of the banging, so I thought that maybe one of the kids had gone into my bedroom unnoticed. I hollered out to Luke and Savannah, and their voices rang in unison from the den... *"What?"* ... hmmm... I sat on the couch frozen for a second, and I have to admit a bit of fear ran through my being. There is something that happens to me when I get scared. First—I get scared, and then after the fear courses through my being for a few moments... I get angry, and the fight and survival mode kicks in!

I called the kids into the living room and told them to follow me into the bedroom, as we were walking into the bedroom, the banging continued and I asked them, *"do you hear that banging?"* They both nodded with a worried look on their faces. We went into my bedroom and stared at my bathroom door as the banging continued. Luke told us that it was a teenage boy on the otherside of the door trying to gain access into our home. This event happened after the migration and we had asked the angels, masters and guides to keep our home clear of any earthbound energy. Well, this teenager was bound and determined to make his way into our home; therefore our angels were providing a protective shield whereby he could not penetrate. Because of this he became angry and kept running into the door in an effort to get through it. He knew he was in a different existence and was earthbound, and was frustrated that he could not simply walk through my bathroom door. I'm not sure how he penetrated the house and made it through into the bathroom. The only thing I have been able to surmise, is the fact that it was our purpose to help him, and the only way possible was if he were to gain entrance into any part of our home.

After a few minutes of standing and staring at the banging door in fear, I became very angry that he had penetrated our shields and gained access to our home. There was a part of me that was angry with the angels for letting him in, as I felt that I should be able to trust that they would keep my space clear if I so asked. In my fit of new found rage and anger I swiftly grabbed the doorknob and with great force I threw the door open and yelled at the top of my lungs. *"What the f--- is your problem?"* My anger was aimed directly toward him and took him back a bit and this put me on top of our fight… this is key when dealing with an angry lost soul. I get a foot hold by using my street smarts and using the art of surprise. Because he was not used to people fighting back I surprised the hell out of him, I was the first human who wouldn't take his crap, and he knew that I was very angry with him.

He had grown accustomed to people being freaked out when he would pull his haunting stunts. He had learned how to use his energies to make noise and banging sounds with physical objects. It didn't help him that he had caught me at a bad time because this was after the migration and we wanted to take a break from all of the earthbound spirits because we were worn out. The problem was that we were too wishy-washy with the angels. Our mouths would say keep them away and then our hearts would feel guilty like we needed to do the work…like there was no one else that could do this. *Yes, we were naive.*

This young boy, who was about seventeen years old, got his groove back on within a few minutes. I went through the normal spill that I always tell them. *"Look"*, I said, *"you're dead, but you're not dead…got it?"* He did not seem all that impressed and I could feel that he thought he was going to take control of the situation. I told him that he was earthbound and that he was finished with his time on this earth and that he needed to make his transition to the other side through the white light. He laughed at me with a smirk on his face and said, *"Oh yeah, what you gonna do, you can't do anything to me!"* I answered him back with, *"Oh yeah?"* and with that I asked Archangel Michael to remove him from our personal space…I told the angels to take his butt to Tennessee for an attitude check, he witnessed and heard the conversation that I had with the angels… and just like that, upon my request, he was swept away in the loving arms of the angels.

I watched tv for a little while longer chuckling inside, thinking things like… *"Hum, I'll show you, you little twit!"* I thought that little punk needed a lesson indeed…scaring me and my kids, oh no… he wasn't gonna get away with that kind of behavior in my home! Once my ego was feed a bit I kindly asked the angels if they would bring him back so that I could get to the business of delivering the important messages to him.

Within a few moments he was back, and humbled. I have to say that he had a pretty good sense of humor, and in a way I think it intrigued him what had taken place. I asked him if he was ready to talk, and if he was, I was there for him. I also told him that he might want to think twice if he was at my home to terrorize me, I told him one more act of rage, and I would send his butt to China!

He agreed that talking was a great idea.

We talked for a few minutes and he asked me questions about the other side and I answered him as best as I could. He really did not have any fear and I knew that he was a pretty cool kid, it's just that he became a bit confused when he died. Within a few minutes he softened and apologized to me and Luke and

Savannah. He listened to us and then he said thank-you and transitioned to the otherside with one of his family members from the otherside who came to take him home.

He was a boy with high self-confidence that could have been misinterpreted as a bad attitude. He was about 6 feet tall with dark blonde hair that was loose curls. His hair was not long, although it kind of hung over his brows and fell at mid-neck, and he had a scar above his right eye. He died in a car wreck with some of his friends. They had been drinking and driving, along with taking other drugs. The car was forest green, and it was a four door. He was a passenger in the back seat. I guess you could say they were joy riding and partying all at the same. He had died early one Sunday morning.

He was very well liked in life, and at school he had friends...he lived in the Midwest in a small farming community, I think it was Iowa. I think that the reason why he was so cocky was that when he died he was drunk and he carried that same energy with him over to his death. He was not used to being drunk because he was young and careless and not so much thinking about the consequences. This partying with his friends was something he would do occasionally, however it was not a weekend habit. He was also ticked off that he was wandering around alone. I think that upon the event of his death he had an immediate awareness that he had died, so he tried to create contact with his mom and dad and two sisters. However, in his mind they just buried him and could no longer see him.

His death hit the family as you would expect...quite hard, he was the second child and he had an older sister who was 23 and a 14 year old little sister. The youngest had the hardest time of it obviously. He was used to getting what he wanted out of life, he was not rich but they were making it okay in the family. He made average grades and had high hopes of going off to college. This was to impress his family but in his heart he was excited to be free as he was a free spirited soul. His name was Nathan.

The story about Nathan is an important one because my experience with him is to show that even though a lost soul may be in an angry or in an aggressive state as an earthbound they are still capable of giving and receiving love. Things can turn around if you but listen to the guidance that you receive. In the case of Nathan I knew that I had to be tough and aggressive right back. But, that was the way to communicate with his soul. Each and every lost soul is different and needs to be treated as such, particularly the ones that I speak of in this chapter.

Rule number one:

When you encounter these earthbounds, don't give them your power by being scared and victimized. You have to treat these lost souls just like you would treat any other person by not allowing them to abuse you. You have the power! You always have the power within you to fight back, so to speak. The way to fight these lost souls is to go toe to toe with them and clear the fear that almost instantly engulfs your physical body the moment you are in their energies. And what I mean by standing toe to toe is that you must stand tall and embrace your self confidence.

The key to self confidence is in knowing that you are a spark of The Divine, and at the same time remembering that they are too. This is extremely hard because some of these lost souls can get quite ornery. Yet, while you stand tall and block their emotions and do not embrace fear of any kind, this melts their anger in a wonderful way. Using the energies of love is much like when you turn on a light in a dark room… the room floods with beautiful light, and all is seen. You have to stand strong and confident for no one wants to neither follow nor heed the words of a weak and scared leader.

When I do the work as a guardian, I have to stay centered and remember that I need to deliver a strong and confident message. These lost souls have to know that you believe in what you are teaching them. In other words, do not feed into their fear—this is what gives them power over you. Also, your fear energies do give them strength and the energy that they need to stay within the lower vibrations. Fear is a powerful emotion on the earth plane. In this line of work, I have to say that these are the souls that require a lot of convincing and talking to because their anger is aimed towards The Divine Creator…Towards God.

Many of these lost souls felt abandoned and angry, they felt that their lives were so bad, therefore, as a defense they fought back and often became the person that was the abuser. Their mentality was to hurt others before others had a chance to hurt them. Therefore, they lashed out with fear and anger hurting many people. Often this was the case because they felt so alone and that no-one had ever loved them. Many of these lost souls were *"thrown away"* in life at a young age. Many of them really did not have anyone to love them. They certainly hated themselves, making it possible for them to hate others to the point of sometimes inflicting physical pain upon others.

We have all been in a place in our lives where we felt these emotions. It's just that some people react in different ways and unfortunately people can get hurt. It really is a sad existence and I feel so much sympathy for them. The sympathy is a key element in helping these lost souls. Sympathy and love is the key, and is one step away from creating understanding, which does bring one closer to finding the love that is hidden deep within the lost soul...and when you find that love, when you find that connection, you will always find the spark of the divine. This is what you are in search of because once you see the spark the soul is ready to make the transition, and since we are all connected, it helps all life to lighten the energy on the earth. We should all care about this because it does affect each and every one of us. We all feel the energies whether we acknowledge them or not.

The lost souls do carry over into their death experience their human emotions of fear, guilt, anger, revenge. Often they think that they have the advantage over you because they can disappear, and then reappear leaving you feeling helpless. This is when the law of your free will comes in. Meaning that when a mischievous soul tries to terrorize you and violate your personal space you can call upon the angels and ascended masters to send the lost soul to kingdom come! You needn't worry about them because the angels know what to do, and they love the lost soul in the same way they love all of us. Try not to think of the earthbound as helpless, because they are the ones trying to invade your space. They are protected and watched over throughout their earthbound existence. All of the angels and masters and guides who were in place for them during their lifetime continue to be with them until they are ready to make their transition home. Just remember that there are laws that govern the universe, and that nothing will ever circumvent your free will. Bottom line is, if you really want them gone... all you have to do is ask and they have to leave, and if they refuse to leave... they will be removed.

There was one guy that we had to ask the angels to remove immediately because his energy was so intense that even Luke could not take it. We did tell the lost soul that he was dead and that he needed to go home through the white light. He had a choice to make, and we did give him the tools and awareness so that possibly down the road if he chose to soften his heart and listen to his angels and guides, he had the knowing and could make the transition sooner than later.

The point to this story is that you can choose to walk away if the situation becomes too much for you. You are indeed protected and the angels are going to always respect your free will and your personal space. You have the power and control to have the earthbound removed from your presence. This is because the earth is primarily for those in the physical. When a person dies they become earthbound because for some reason or another the lost soul chose to stay on the earth, however it is not their natural domain.

We have learned through the school of hard knocks that we will never go and seek the lost soul out. We are not ghost hunters. We are here to answer the call of God and the angels and when we are willing, they bring those souls to us. I have much faith in the fact that there is purpose in all of the souls who are brought to us. There is much that I do not know about what goes on behind the scenes which can even take many earth years before the soul is brought to us. Yet, I have learned to have faith and trust that there is something bigger than me at work here.

It is easy to let the ego step in a take control and because of that I think that it is important for guardians to keep in mind that this is Gods work and that it is sacred. These lost souls that we choose to help are people too, they are mothers, sisters, brothers, fathers and someone's best friend. They are real and it is important to respect that we are helping them get back home to Mother-Father God, their families and loved ones.

The power that I was talking about earlier is important. When you are in your own space, your home, your car, the earthbound spirit is bound by the laws of the universe and that is the first law of free will. Don't expect the same courtesy to be afforded to you if you go into the lost soul's domain. Ghost hunters are on their own—basically. It's not that I don't think that people can't help in spaces that aren't their own domain, it's just that if you do invade; you have to realize that you are going to them, you are invading their space, and if they refuse your help to make the transition, you need to leave. Many guardians are successful in helping lost souls make the transition and work diligently and go to many places to help the lost soul.

Another thing to keep in mind is if you buy a home that they once owned and died in, well, I guess you had better understand that you may have a cranky and oftentimes noisy guest that will live with you until they are ready to leave. This is because they feel as though you have invaded their space and do not like this at all.

A public place is a neutral territory, therefore the angels help the one who is most in need at the time, whether it be the lost soul or the person who is in the physical body.

The angels who are Gods messengers do work as an extension of The Divine Creators will. The angels are the ones who do the mass amount of the work in the spaces in-between, they do know all and they do hear your pleas for help. If you are asking a mischievous soul to leave but in your heart you want them to stay, the angels will not remove them. However, and this is the greatest part of all, if you want the earthbound removed from your space all you have to do is ask and it will be done. I used to feel guilty and worry about where the soul was being sent, but then I remembered that the angels have love and respect for all of Gods children and do treat them with kindness and love.

There is a plan to all that is—in this beautiful world. The key to helping the lost soul make the transition is to call upon legions of angels and keep love and light in your home, this is the elixir that will wake them from their slumber. When working with the light and love of The Divine you must treat the lost soul as you would any other person in the skin who is ill and needs medication. The medication for the lost soul is the love and light of Christ and the eternal knowing that all is well.

Chapter 10

Harold, Somewhere in Time

There are many times that we are experiencing things that at the time we are beside ourselves with fear and really don't know how it is we are going to get through it. Then we are filled with anger and rage because of the fear. The story of Harold is just the story that changed the way I think about earthbound people. I had a knowing that I was dealing with real people, who had real lives, but I had managed to turn my emotions off to it pretty well, that is until Harold. Harold touched my soul on a deep level because of his love and caring towards my daughter Savannah.

I was on the back porch grouting the tile. We had been working on construction on the house for some time and I was desperately trying to bring it to completion. This was not an easy task as we were swarming with earthbounds and every time I turned around Savannah was running to me in fear and wanting me to talk to them to cross them over. I was becoming irritated with the constant interruptions to my workday, so much so, that I am embarrassed to admit, I was kind of cold to some of the earthbound people that were coming to us. I would coldly say, *"You're dead so go to the light"*. Thankfully, for some of them, that method actually worked pretty well! I know that the angels and God were quite tuned into my mood…therefore I believe that in those times they were bringing those to me that needed the ice-cold treatment in order to make their transitions. However, some of these earthbound people had many questions and wanted to know what was going on in their lives. I say lives because for them they were still living their lives. For many it had been quite some time since someone in the flesh had noticed their presence, so they would want for conversation and answers to what was going on.

Nevertheless, as they had been coming in at that time, I was spending five minutes working and 30 minutes or so talking to the earthbounds. I was spending much of my time leading them home through the light. This was about a week or so before the migration when they began gradually streaming in larger numbers and more frequently. Within a couple of weeks they went from one a day, to several in a day. I remember thinking how overwhelming it was when we got three at the same time. *How little I knew, because I had no idea as to what was about to happen with the migration!*

This particular afternoon I had given Savannah the chore to mop the kitchen floor. I was determined that our house was going to be in order. Savannah came running out to the back porch, her face was flushed and she told me that there was a guy following her around. I was not in the mood at the time, therefore I told her to go back into the house and complete her chores. I told her that we could not use the lost souls as an excuse not to do the things in our lives that were important to us.

I told her that it was important to remember that we are in the physical and our lives, and the things we do were just as important as helping lost souls. Therefore, I told her to ignore him so that he would go away. I remember thinking that I was not going to be the neighborhood ghost-buster on call 24/7.

She went back into the house and within a few moments she was back out on the back porch with tears in her eyes and she was very scared and upset. Frustrated and cursing under my breath, I went into the house to search for this guy and give him a piece of my mind. When I found him I ordered him out to the back porch with me, I was not about to stop working, therefore he would have to listen to what I had to say while I was grouting the tile. He followed me outside and once we got outside I let him know that it was not very nice at all to scare my little girl and that he was in my house, not his, and that he must leave. But then something happened to me while I was letting him have it…I felt him. He was crying and was sincerely sorry, he told me that he in no way ever wanted to scare Savannah. I felt his loving spirit immediately and it was all I could do to hold back the tears myself. He told us that he was so happy that someone had finally seen him.

While Savannah was in the house he noticed that she saw him and because he was so excited he went running up to her proclaiming *"you see me, you see me!"* and he rushed up to her so quickly that it nearly scared her half to death. When she tried to ignore him he did not give up, he kept getting in her face proclaiming that he had finally been seen. He was one of her scarier earthbound moments. When I told Harold that he had scared Savannah into crying, he started to cry because it broke his heart that he had scared her.

Once I realized that he was gentle soul, I spoke to him in a calm and loving manner. I apologized to him for being so crash and cranky, but that I was just trying to get some work done around the house—I also told him that I don't like it when Savannah gets scared. He told me that it was okay and that he was sorry too.

We explained to him that it was important that he make his transition to the otherside through the white light. I also told him that he was welcome anytime to visit once he was in spirit form and that if he would like, he could come back and help us with some of the earthbound spirits once he had made the transition back home.

He had asked me if there was anything that he could do to help pay us back and I told him that I would love to have his help from the otherside, he said that he would love to help in any way he could. It only took about five minutes of conversation with him before he crossed over. To our delight he sent a postcard from heaven to us rather quickly, he loved the band acdc and his favorite song was Back in Black. All of the sudden we heard this song playing through the energies… it was beautiful!

Harold was a beautiful black man, and he was in his early 30s, he died of liver cancer. He had been sick for quite some time. He was married with a child. He was the most loving earthbound spirit that I have ever been around.

I realize now that the timing of them bringing Harold to us was impeccable, along with some of the other earthbound spirits at that time in preparation for what we were about to experience with the migration. Harold came and helped us tremendously during the migration and even today we will call on him when we have a particularly difficult lost soul to deal with.

He is such a joy and we always know when he is around because we hear the song Back in Black through the energies...it is his calling card, so to speak.

Now, we have a whole host of helpers from heaven. They are so willing to come and help us when we need it. They are the perfect help as they truly understand the earthbound state because they had experienced it themselves. The former lost souls help us to communicate and they talk to the earthbound spirits who come our way. It is nice to know that we have these heavenly helpers to rely on when there is a tough moment in trying to get some obstinate soul to make the transition.

These souls who were formerly earthbound are very grateful and it usually does not take them long before they are their old selves once again and are able to us help in a way as to ease our load. There have been times that all we have to do is to call for their help, and then when they get here, they do all the talking to the earthbound spirit. They have all of the right words to say and there have been times when they have come in to help fellow earthbounds whom they knew while they were in that state themselves.

Harold has brought many lost souls in need of help to us. And between all of us, we create a beautiful communication with the lost soul. The lost soul can' communicate with Harold and us at the same time. They are often surprised to hear that he was also earthbound after he died.

It is a busy place...the spaces in-between. The angels, masters, guides and spirits from the otherside are helping to locate and round up lost souls to help them and assist them to make the transition home. Sometimes they simply need someone like us, in the flesh to do the talking. It seems as though we offer some sort of credibility to the lost souls. They are in such a dream state like existence that they need someone or something that is tangible. It seems as if we kind of pull them back into our reality which in turn opens their heart and soul to receive the truth. Imagine, of you will, being in a dream state that continues to loop endlessly and that you are stuck in the same scene over and over again...not unlike the movie Groundhog Day. But then something happens and someone different comes into the dream to help you realize that there is something not quite right. This is often the key to awaken the lost soul from their dream state... us!

Only a former earthbound can truly comprehend this state of being, thus, making them the perfect candidate to help with this process of finding and helping all of the lost souls back home. Many former lost souls are now guardians, and they work their mission as guardians of lost souls with beauty and grace and tremendous success. I have a prayer of gratitude in my heart at all times for these beautiful souls who have touched my life.

Harold, I love you dear friend...

See you on the other side, and thanks for all you have done and do for the many lost souls and guardians.

Chapter 11

Post Cards from Heaven

Post Cards from Heaven by: Savannah at age 11

"*Post cards from heaven are pretty much a little thank you note. They show me millions of different things from weird to funny. When I first discovered this was when I saw a giant monster cookie, for some reason they send mostly food and flowers. Sometimes I get a postcard that reflects some of their favorite things. Sometimes they send me postcards of things I love. They are usually from the ones that I was scared and they wanted to help me feel better, and it did. One of my most memorable post card was a giant rose garden on the wall in my living room. It was sent by a group, we did a group crossing. The post cards sent by the people are like a vision that I get but I know that it is from them because many times they are standing next to it with a proud smile on their face. It is a gift of love from them to me. I really do love the postcards. It lightens my load, and helps me understand that they are just people like me and have feelings too. Sometimes the postcards will come with a scent. There was one time when I saw the sugar cookies, and* then I smelt them.   He sent me that postcard because it was a found memory of his mother who baked sugar cookies for him. He told me that.   That was one of the best ways that he could send his love to me was by a feeling that created much love and warmth in his heart.

I love getting the post cards because I learn something special about them every time.

She had a red butterfly shirt, blue eyes and brown hair. She was scared but we talked to her and helped her understand what was going on. We live on a lake, and we were talking to her on our back screened in porch. After she crossed over, I looked out over the lake and noticed a huge can as big as the oak tree of spagettios spewing over the side of the can into the lake. She told me when she came back that she loved spagettios and that is why she sent that post card to me. I loved it because I even got the smell of spagettios; it was almost as if I was eating giant five foot wide rings of spagettios."

Pennies from Heaven

When I was a little girl our family would travel to visit my grandpa. He was of humble means and he always saved every penny he earned. His money was always well spent. He would collect his pennies and save them in mason jars so that he could give the jars of pennies to his grandkids. I remember how much fun it was to go through the pennies and count them, look at the dates, and fantasize about all of the different places around our world the pennies had traveled.

It has been many years since my grandpa has passed, and he has always acted as a guardian angel of sorts for me. He gets great joy out of sending me pennies in many different ways. One day as I was walking into the grocery store, a penny fell out of the sky right in front of me out of thin air and slammed onto the ground. I picked it up and smiled because I knew that he was sending me a message—that he loved me. *I love it when he does that.*

One day when I was walking on the beach I looked down into the water and there was a penny, I knew once again that it was a gift from grandpa. I then jokingly said to him..."*what are the odds that I will get another penny*"; I giggled to myself because I knew that he would produce another one for me. Sure enough about a half mile later, I looked down and there it was—barely peeking out from the sand under the water...another penny.

The pennies that he sends me have different messages on each one of them. For instance the dates on the pennies are significant, and he speaks in many ways to me through the messages and symbols on the pennies. This is a fun game that we have with one-another. If you were to come into my house you would see pennies here and there, the kids know to leave them be because they are *pennies from heaven.*

One time one of my friends told me that I should ask him to bring me hundred dollar bills, but I said no way. It is not about the money...it is the meaning behind it, our experiences and the fun way he brings them to me.

Otis and the Choo-Choo Train

One night during the migration we helped a lost soul named Otis. He was interesting in the fact that he was blind, and still had his guide dog with him. She was a beautiful German Sheppard. He was a quiet soul, and was simply wandering around. He did not know that he was dead, therefore in his death experience he was still blind and created the manifestation of his guide dog. This is the beauty of The Divine in that no one is ever left alone, the angels brought him to us so that we could deliver the message to him, and "wake him" from his earthbound dream state.

We learned very little about him, although he told us that when he was a little boy he loved choo-choo trains... he said he just loved the sounds that the trains made. We talked with him for a few minutes and delivered the message to him that it was time to go to heaven. He was thrilled to move on, and asked us if he would be able to see in heaven, of course we told him that absolutely he would be able to see when he went to heaven. Several minutes after he made his transition home, all of the sudden it was as if the ground started to vibrate and then out of nowhere we heard the sounds of a locomotive racing between our house and our neighbors house.

We looked up and around and then we heard the loud whistle of the train... We sat speechless staring at one another, and Luke, Savannah and I all said at once to each other *"Did you hear that!"* we all said *"YES!!!"* We were speechless and laughing all at once. It was a most beautiful spiritual experience, we told Otis thank you and that we loved his post card from heaven. It was interesting because he did not give us the manifestation of a vision or being able to see the train. He was sharing his experience that he had while he was alive, feeling and hearing the train. Now, anytime I hear a train I think of my loving and dear friend Otis.

A Butterfly from My lady

Several days after Katherine had crossed over I was sitting on my back porch lost in thought. I was still in a place where I felt tremendous emotional turmoil from the events of the night when she first came to me. I felt her presence come in around me and she told me not to worry, and that everything would be alright. I told her she was sweet, and that I was grateful that she was in a better place, however, I asked her if she would give me some time because when she came around me it brought me back to the energies and visions of her earthbound dream. She was loving and caring and told me she did understand. As she left I looked up and saw the most beautiful butterfly fluttering by. The colors of the butterfly were not of this world...they were of a heavenly vibration. I knew the butterfly was her post card from heaven to me. It was so beautiful and dainty with light colors of coral. Since then, whenever I feel her presence, I take a look around me and sure enough, I see the beautiful butterfly... her post card from heaven for me.

Meetings on the Other-Side

One afternoon, Luke, Savannah and I were lying down doing a meditation and just clearing our bodies, which was badly needed. During the meditation Savannah bolted up and said *"Mom, I was in a room full of all of the people we crossed over, there were so many that I was floating above them and it seemed as they went on forever!"*…she was so excited. Then later in the meditation she told me that she went through a white light, into a room full of people. At first it really freaked her out because all of the sudden she thought she had crossed over and she did not want to leave me. She said that she could see her body and was going in and out of the light. She was fidgeting right next to me so I tapped her on her shoulder and she said she slammed back into her body. Within a few minutes Luke spoke up and told us that he was on a beach riding a horse then he wound up in a building, he said he saw books and people. He was excited. Savannah told me that when she went through the light she saw a case that in it there was a gold book with paper thin gold pages, she started to read some but that was when I nudged her, so we don't know what it said. I think they found themselves in the same room at different times. The post cards from heaven in this story were the souls that greeted and talked to Luke and Savannah.

Post cards from heaven come in many different forms, sometimes they are simply messages of gratitude and thank-you's from loved ones, and it is an extra bonus when you can see and talk to the ones who are sending the messages of love!

Before, during and after the migration we received literally hundreds of post cards from heaven from the loving souls who made the transition home. Just like Savannah said, it really did seem to *"lighten our load"*.

Everyone gets post cards from heaven. All one must do is take a look around and notice. Sometimes the postcards from heaven will come through messages in the clouds... it happens suddenly. The clouds will form beautiful shapes and forms that are messages from our loved ones, and we always seem to know what the message is. Another form of post cards from heaven is music that is played on the radio. These are messages that touch our hearts through the words that are sung and offer the reminder that someone on the otherside is reaching out and telling us that they love us.

When you see these post cards, and all of the sudden you think about a loved one who has gone home, know that your loved one is thinking about you too...sending you loving messages from heaven!

Appendix

Afterword

Two years have passed since the events of this book... Much in our life has changed as we have progressed and grown. We have learned much about the art of setting boundaries and limits with the spaces in-between, thus, our home and personal space vibrate on a high heavenly energy of angels, masters and guides. There are the occasional lost souls who come our way, and we do help them... if we feel that it is necessary, however, we have learned that it is important that we say no, if needs be.

Savannah is living her love and taking horse riding lessons and we feel indeed blessed by the opportunity that has come into her life. She has even competed in a few dressage competitions, winning ribbons in both. Luke has just recently passed the test to get his learners permit and is very excited about learning how to drive, and he is looking forward to doing some volunteer work this coming year at the local zoo. He wants to be a herpetologist when he grows up.

I would like to say thank you so much to my husband David who has been through many ups and downs with me...yet, he is still here...still loving me, no matter what! I love you honey.

To Piper, what would we have done without your beautiful and loving guidance? Thank you so much for being a bright light in the darkest of times. "It's me and the kids!" We Love you!

Contact Information:

Pamela

www.guardianoflostsouls.com

Joan Piper

www.joanpiper.com

Coming Soon! More Books by Pamela:

Guardian of Lost Souls – Lessons in Life

Guardian of Lost Souls – Coming Together

Who's Wrong with Me? An Empath's Guide

Made in the USA
Lexington, KY
27 April 2010

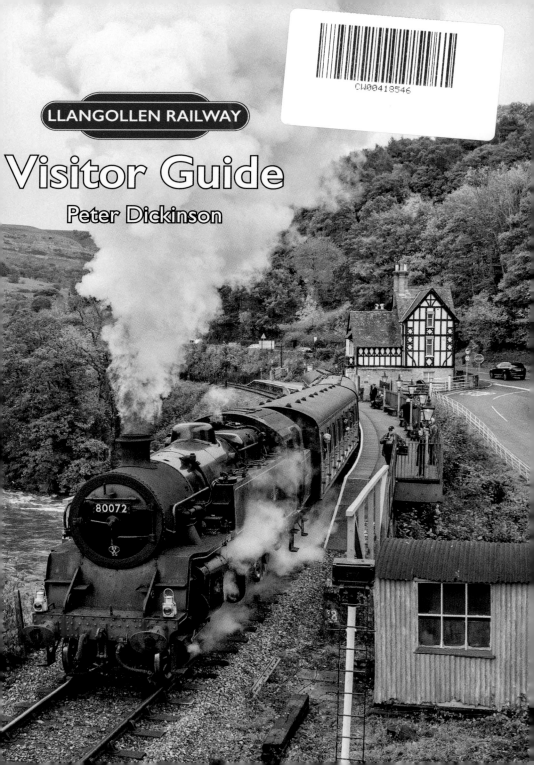

LLANGOLLEN RAILWAY

Visitor Guide

Peter Dickinson

80072

Welcome

Stepping onboard one of the Llangollen Railway's trains is a ticket to your own personal railway adventure.

The Llangollen Railway, a true country line of the old Great Western Railway, was opened more than 150 years ago and offers a nostalgic ride back in time. The historic steam and diesel locomotives transport passengers from Llangollen, the riverside town where 'Wales welcomes the World', to the picturesque market town of Corwen.

Along the way, the railway remains close to the tumbling waters of the River Dee, with the whole line being within an Area of Outstanding Natural Beauty (AONB). The gently rolling hills, unspoilt villages, farms nestling in leafy lanes, the beautiful Valle Crucis Abbey and an internationally renowned World Heritage Site are all waiting to be discovered.

Once ubiquitous workhorses in their day, heritage steam locomotives are now historic survivors and attract quite a following in their own right. Great Western Railway 'Small Prairie' tank No 4566 awaits the green flag from the guard to proceed from Berwyn station back towards Llangollen. *Clive Hanley*

The five unique stations linked by the 10-mile scenic journey offer the perfect starting points to further explore the Dee Valley and will repay hours of exploration. This guidebook will be the perfect companion for you to make the most of your visit to the Llangollen Railway and the wider Dee Valley.

The history of the preserved Llangollen Railway is the story of a colossal struggle to keep a dying part of Britain's heritage alive, a struggle that still goes on today. The Railway was once part of a cross-country route linking the coalfields of Ruabon in the east with the seaside resort of Barmouth in the west. The route developed into an important artery across rural Wales, bringing in its wake a revolution in agriculture, industry and daily life. Seasonal holiday traffic became big business, tapping into the expanding conurbations of Liverpool, Manchester and Birmingham.

However, the influx of cars, lorries and buses on Britain's roads soon made the railway a liability rather than a vital service in the eyes of the Government, and after a century of service the line was closed. The railway tracks were lifted and the surviving infrastructure began to decay. This is where the battle to preserve the Llangollen Railway began.

Starting in 1975, a small band of enthusiasts set about restoring and rebuilding a section of the railway from the derelict Llangollen station, setting their sights on the next town of Corwen. Despite facing many challenges and obstacles, heritage trains returned to the Dee Valley and once again link the two towns.

The story does not end there. The Llangollen Railway continues to develop its services and expand, and with the invaluable help of its staff and volunteers, will hopefully continue to do so for many years to come.

- Virtually everyone you meet during your visit is a volunteer, from station staff and signalmen to guards and locomotive crews.
- It takes up to 4 hours for our loco crews to prepare one of our historic steam locomotives in the morning and another hour to 'dispose' of the loco at the end of the day. Work in the morning includes lighting and building up the fire, coaling up, checking over the loco, oiling and cleaning ready for the day ahead.
- When working on the railway, each steam locomotive can cost as much as £1,000 per day. Our engines use between 3 and 4 tonnes of coal each day – approximately the same weight as an average hippopotamus.
- The railway is supported by an army of around 200 active volunteers.
- Our volunteers come from a wide spectrum of disciplines including carpenters, bricklayers, electrical engineers, geologists, painters, mechanics, upholsterers, health and safety professionals, accountants and teachers, as well as many with experience in IT, social media, administration and catering.
- We are overseen by the Office of Rail and Road (ORR) and the Rail Accident Investigation Branch (RAIB), which ensure that the railway is run in a professional manner.
- On the majority of our services, passengers will find themselves seated in British Railways Mark I carriages – a design dating back to the 1950s and early 1960s.
- We are responsible for 20 miles of fencing and drainage channels.
- On our first open day back in 1975, we only had 60 feet of track laid in Llangollen station, but attracted 1,500 visitors.

The sweeping curves and wooded hillsides are a feature of the line around Glyndyfrdwy village. London Midland & Scottish Railway-designed locomotive No 44806 approaches the station with a westbound service. *Clive Hanley*

A place where time has seemingly stood still. Carrog station has been meticulously restored back to its 1950s condition and provided the setting for this evening photographic charter with 1953-built locomotive No 80072. *Dave Bowles*

Your ticket to explore

Llangollen

Llangollen station is the headquarters of our railway and houses our offices and workshops. The station is located alongside the famous 13th-century **Llangollen Bridge** over the River Dee (much widened in the following centuries). Our station platforms are a well-known suntrap, ideal for drinking tea and watching the world go by!

Llangollen was a major coaching stop for the Irish Mail on Thomas Telford's main road from London to Holyhead. With the arrival of the railway in 1862, the town prospered from the regular influxes of tourists and holidaymakers.

The historic Plas Newydd was the home of the 'Ladies of Llangollen', Lady Eleanor Butler and Sarah Ponsonby, for nearly 50 years, and was converted into their Gothic 'fantasy'. *Peter Dickinson*

Llangollen Wharf is the starting point for relaxing canal boat trips throughout the season towards the Horseshoe Falls and the Pontcysyllte Aqueduct. *Peter Dickinson*

The charming historic streets of the town are worthy of further exploration. *Peter Dickinson*

Nowadays you will find plenty of independent shops to browse and interesting places to visit. Take a stroll along the **Victorian Promenade**, picnic in the **Riverside Park** or even try your hand at crazy golf.

Local attractions include the **Llangollen Museum** celebrating the history of the town and **Plas Newydd**, the home of the 'Ladies of Llangollen'.

Overlooking the town are the impressive and imposing remains of **Dinas Bran Castle**, which was built in the 1260s by a local Welsh ruler, Prince Gruffudd ap Madoc, to guard the strategic route through the Dee Valley. Although little remains of this once great castle, it is well worth the steep climb for the spectacular views over Llangollen and the surrounding countryside below.

In 1884 a horse-drawn passenger boat service for sightseers started on the town's canal. It is still possible to enjoy a slow meander along the canal from **Llangollen Wharf**, located just a short walk above our railway station.

Berwyn

Situated in a prominent position beside Thomas Telford's main London to Holyhead road, Berwyn station is instantly recognisable due to its distinctive appearance. The half-timbered Tudor appearance of the station was designed to match the adjacent **Chain Bridge Hotel** at the request of a local landowner.

The station is ideal for walkers – see our *Walks from the Railway* book for suggestions of walks in the area. The **Horseshoe Falls**, built by Thomas Telford to act as a feeder for the Llangollen Canal, is just a 15-minute walk from the station.

Alternatively, you may decide to head in the opposite direction along the canal and return to Llangollen (30-40 minutes). The **Llangollen Motor Museum**, **Valle Crucis Abbey** and **Llantysilio Church** are all within walking distance.

The Horseshoe Falls was built to act as a feeder for the Llangollen Canal and has been attracting visitors since its opening in the early 1800s. Follow in the footsteps of Queen Victoria, as she once stayed in one of the large houses overlooking the Falls and took tea there during a Royal visit. *Russell Dunn*

Berwyn station is linked to the adjacent canal and hotel by one of the first chain bridges in the world. This famous **Chain Bridge** was originally built in 1813 by a local coal merchant to open up a transport route across the River Dee – avoiding paying the toll in Llangollen in the process!

It is worth pausing to investigate the walls of the pedestrian underpass while taking the footpath down from Berwyn's platform to the Chain Bridge. The white glazed bricks seem to have taken pencil markings readily, particularly the indelible type issued to soldiers during the First World War. Local teenage conscripts used their pencils to write messages and notes on the walls as the footpath passed under the railway line. Some of the surviving messages include 'Balls from Belgium', 'Berlin Last Stop', 'Hoof Hearted' and, rather poignantly, 'I really want this baby'.

Glyndyfrdwy

The meandering Llangollen Canal offers the perfect opportunity to stretch your legs and explore the sylvan Dee Valley further.
Peter Dickinson

Glyndyfrdwy station represents the start of the railway's entry into the homeland of Owain Glyndwr. It was here in September 1400, as Lord of the Manor, that he raised his standard in revolt against the English Crown. With a small band of supporters, he took the title of Prince of Wales, and went on to fight many battles in his long and epic struggle against the English. The **Owain Glyndwr Memorial Hall**, just a short walk from the station, contains artefacts associated with him.

Breaking your journey at Glyndyfrdwy offers the opportunity to enjoy the **tranquil picnic areas** that the station offers, take a stroll down to the nearby River Dee or around the village. The village's **playing field and play area** adjoining the station are very popular with young families.

For the more adventurous, the station is the ideal starting

The village of Glyndyfrdwy provides the ideal starting point from which to explore the wild North Berwyn Mountains, taking in rich woodland and expansive moorland along the way.
Peter Dickinson

point for walkers exploring the wild North Berwyn Mountains to the south of the line. The waymarked **North Berwyn Way** is a challenging route for experienced walkers, while the former Nant y Pandy tramway offers a less strenuous climb through woodland up to open moorland and disused slate quarries. See our *Walks from the Railway* book for details of this and other suggestions for walks in the area.

During some of our special events throughout the year, the field behind the station building is transformed into a showground and plays host to many vintage buses, cars and motorbikes.

Carrog

Carrog station is located on the opposite bank of the river from its namesake village. Linking the two is the 17th-century Carrog Bridge, which gracefully spans the River Dee with its five stone arches. In 1601 the ferocity of the flooding on the Dee swept away the Church of St Bridget, the remains of which are believed to be in the riverbed some 200 yards downstream of the current bridge.

The village was originally called Llansantffraid-Glyndyfrdwy until the arrival of the railway in the 1860s. It was renamed 'Carrog' using the name of a local manor house to avoid confusion. Rows of large Victorian and Edwardian houses were built as holiday homes by wealthy Liverpool families after the opening of the railway. Today the village still enjoys a regular influx of visitors, mainly due to the large **campsite** adjacent to the station.

The quaint and well-spoken-of **Grouse Inn** is just a short walk away and offers panoramic views down onto the river, as well as an extensive menu of home-cooked food.

Carrog station is frequently used as a venue for our special events and is transformed every winter into 'Lapland' as part of our 'Santa Specials'. Volunteer locomotive groups use the station's former sidings and cattle dock area as a venue for their **fundraising shops** in vintage carriages. The Railway's Heritage Group has installed its newly restored **Pooley Van** alongside Carrog's signal box, offering displays of the line's history and current restoration projects.

Carrog Bridge is just a short walk from the station, with the well-spoken-of Grouse Inn beyond.
Peter Dickinson

Corwen

Corwen is often referred to as the 'crossroads of North Wales' and has roots that go back into the mists of time. The town was a centre for cattle drovers and a favourite with Victorian travellers. Its name means 'the White Choir' or 'White Church', referring to the church founded here by the 6th-century Saints Mael and Sulien.

The Iron Age fort of **Caer Drewyn** on the hill to the north of the town has been witness to the often-violent history of the Dee Valley from Roman times through to the medieval campaigns of the English Kings. Legend suggests that when local nobleman Owain Gwynedd proclaimed himself King of Wales in the 10th century, he gathered his forces at the fort while he waited for the approach of Henry II's English army.

Before the railway arrived in Corwen in the 1860s, the town was a changeover point for horse-drawn vehicles on Thomas Telford's main road from London to Holyhead.

The little market town also has strong connections with Owain Glyndwr, who is celebrated by a **statue** in the town square and the name of a hotel in his honour. The hotel has a fascinating past, with the earliest part of the building believed to date from 1329.

Nowadays the **Corwen Museum** is the perfect starting point for visitors wishing to learn more about the culture and heritage of the town and the surrounding Dee Valley. The former **Victorian Workhouse** opposite the museum has been converted into a craft shop selling candles made on the premises, clothing and fishing tackle.

Since 2012 Corwen has been an accredited **'Walkers are Welcome'** town and hosts an annual Walking Festival. For anyone wishing to go on and explore one of Britain's lost railways, the trackbed of the line onwards from Corwen to the next village of Cynwyd is now a popular footpath and **local nature reserve**. See our *Walks from the Railway* book for details of this and other suggestions for walks in the area.

The impressive statue of Owain Glyndwr in the centre of Corwen's town square.
Peter Dickinson

Timeline

- **1859** – Parliamentary authority is obtained to build the Vale of Llangollen Railway from Ruabon to Llangollen.
- **1860** – Parliamentary authority is obtained to build the Llangollen & Corwen Railway.
- **1862** – First passenger trains arrive at Llangollen from Ruabon.
- **1865** – First passenger trains commence between Llangollen and Corwen.
- **1896** – The Llangollen & Corwen Railway is fully absorbed into the Great Western Railway.
- **1897-1900** – Major upgrade of the railway includes expansion of Llangollen station and installation of new signal boxes.
- **1948** – Upon nationalisation, the Great Western Railway becomes part of British Railways (Western Region).
- **1965** – BR passenger service through Llangollen and Corwen cease.
- **1967-68** – Railway track along the line is lifted and some buildings are demolished by BR contractors.
- **1975** – First public open day at Llangollen Station, marking start of Llangollen Railway's preservation scheme.
- **1981** – First Llangollen Railway (LR) passenger trains in preservation depart from Llangollen station.
- **1986** – LR passenger services are extended to Berwyn.
- **1990** – LR passenger services are extended through Berwyn Tunnel to Deeside Halt.
- **1992** – LR passenger services are extended to Glyndyfrdwy; line is now 5¼ miles long.
- **1996** – LR passenger services are extended to Carrog.
- **2014** – First passenger service into Corwen commences, using temporary platform at Dwyrain Corwen East.
- **2019** – Trackwork completed into LR's new western terminus of Corwen Central.

The birth of a railway

The idea of building a railway to connect Llangollen with Britain's rapidly expanding railway network was first mooted in 1845. Several proposals were considered before Royal Assent (Parliamentary approval) was given to the Vale of Llangollen Railway Bill of 1859. This document enabled 5 miles of railway to be constructed from a junction south of Ruabon, on the Shrewsbury to Chester route, through the villages of Acrefair and Trevor to the eastern outskirts of Llangollen.

The construction contract for this first section was awarded to the contractor Thomas Brassey, who had previously overseen many railway building projects including the Grand Trunk Railway across Canada. The Scottish mining engineer and prolific railway builder Henry Robertson was appointed as Chief Engineer. Despite meteorological and financial problems, construction proceeded rapidly and was completed in 1862.

The Vale of Llangollen Railway opened to much celebration by local people on 2 June 1862, with hundreds congregating at the railway's Vicarage Terminus in Llangollen to witness the inauguration of the passenger service. Expansion plans for the line were already afoot; the Llangollen & Corwen Railway Bill had received Parliamentary approval in 1860 and construction was already under way. This new 10-mile section of line westwards from Llangollen would terminate in the town of Corwen, passing through the villages of Glyndyfrdwy and Carrog, while also serving a series of large private residences around Berwyn.

The original layout of Llangollen station is shown to good effect in this view from around 1895. Following the GWR's takeover the following year, the station was heavily modified to incorporate longer platforms, a new footbridge and additional station buildings. *Peter Dickinson collection*

By far the biggest engineering challenge on the Llangollen & Corwen Railway was the 689-yard (630-metre) Berwyn Tunnel. This shortened the railway by about 3 miles and removed the need for some sharp curves had the course of the River Dee been closely followed. Work began at either end of the tunnel in 1862 and when the two sections met in late 1864 there was only a slight difference in alignments.

The Llangollen & Corwen Railway opened to the public in May 1865, with temporary stations being used in both towns until completion of permanent facilities in the autumn. Further extensions promoted by the Great Western Railway (GWR) took the new line closer to the Cambrian Coast, reaching Bala and Dolgelly (sic) by 1868. However, hopes of the GWR reaching the resort of Barmouth by its own metals were thwarted when a rival railway company built a branch to Dolgelly. The GWR then had to obtain running powers to enable its trains to reach the coast.

From the outset, the four individual railway companies operating the line between Ruabon and Dolgelly never owned their own locomotives or rolling stock, these being hired from and maintained by the GWR.

The Great Western takeover

The later years of the Victorian era were a period of many railway amalgamations and absorptions, and unsurprisingly the Ruabon to Dolgelly line was no exception. The GWR took the opportunity to absorb the series of independent railway companies in 1896, bringing the majority of the route under its control. The remaining section between Barmouth and Dolgelly (spelled 'Dolgelley' from 1895) continued to be independent until it too was absorbed by the GWR in 1923.

The GWR began to make some major improvements to its new line almost immediately. Between 1897 and 1900 the section between Ruabon and Llangollen was doubled to cope with the increasing passenger and goods traffic, while Llangollen station was expanded in size. New halts were constructed to optimise passenger traffic and a new passing loop opened at Deeside in 1908 to break up the 5-mile single-line section between Llangollen and Glyndyfrdwy.

GWR 'Dukedog' Class Nos 9017 and 9021 pause for water at Corwen with an excursion in April 1958. *Peter Dickinson collection*

The Barmouth to Dolgellau shuttle service arrives at Penmaenpool station in 1964. The westernmost section of the cross-Wales route has been reincarnated as the Mawddach Trail footpath and cycleway alongside the estuary. *Peter Dickinson collection*

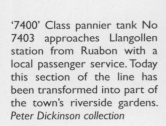

Nationalisation and decline

Nationalisation of the British railway network on 1 January 1948 placed the Ruabon to Barmouth line in the ownership of the Western Region of the newly formed British Railways (BR). Initially the line continued in very much the same way as it had previously under GWR ownership. However, by the start of the 1950s the increasing ownership of family cars became one of the factors in the decline of rural railways.

BR regional boundary changes saw the route come under London Midland Region control on 1 January 1963. By then the writing was on the wall, and the following October saw the first closure notices posted for the line. The closure process rumbled on well into 1964, with the provisional January closure date being missed and a series of consultations taking place. The final date for closure of the Ruabon to Barmouth line was chosen to be in January 1965.

Overnight on 12 and 13 December 1964 the line was severely damaged by flooding, with around 20 metres of embankment washed away near Bala, and further damage sustained around Corwen, Glyndyfrdwy and Llangollen. Train services were soon restored on the Ruabon

to Llangollen and the Bala to Barmouth sections, but the damage to the Corwen to Bala section was deemed too great to repair and a replacement bus service was provided between Llangollen and Bala. The last timetabled passenger trains on the line ran on 16 January 1965, although goods services between Llangollen and Ruabon lingered on until 1968.

The majority of the disused track along the line was lifted by demolition contractors during 1968. Nature then took over, stations became derelict and the trackbed overgrown. The closure could have signalled the end of the railway's story, but a dedicated group of enthusiasts would ensure that full-sized trains could once again be seen in the Dee Valley.

'7400' Class pannier tank No 7403 approaches Llangollen station from Ruabon with a local passenger service. Today this section of the line has been transformed into part of the town's riverside gardens.
Peter Dickinson collection

BR Standard No 75021 passes Bryn Howel, roughly midway between Ruabon and Llangollen, during the summer of 1964. *Peter Dickinson collection*

LMS Ivatt No 46508 enters Berwyn Halt in 1964. By this time the once grand station building had been closed and replaced by a simple wooden shelter on the platform. *Peter Dickinson collection*

A blanket of snow covers the Dee Valley. *Richard Smith*

The 1960s in colour

Berwyn station in the summer of 1965 following closure. *Peter Dickinson collection*

BR Standard No 75026 approaches Glyndyfrdwy in April 1964 with a Barmouth to Birkenhead service. *Peter Dickinson collection*

BR-built Pannier Tank No 1628 heads a short eastbound goods train in the railway cutting at Bryn Howel in 1964 *Peter Dickinson collection*.

The very last passenger train (an enthusiasts' special) passes through Llangollen station in April 1967 prior to tracklifting. *Peter Dickinson collection*

Rebirth of the railway

Llangollen was fortunate as there was an embryonic and growing preservation movement developing throughout Britain. One group, the Flint & Deeside Railway Preservation Society, which aspired to the restoration and preservation of a standard-gauge line, decided that Llangollen was ideal. The section of line between Llangollen and Corwen, containing the intermediate stations of Berwyn, Glyndyfrdwy and Carrog, was their focus for restoration.

The trackbed and stations had been purchased by the local council, but, realising the potential of a major tourist attraction being developed, they willingly leased the station and 3 miles of track to what was to become the Llangollen Railway Trust.

The railway's closure had resulted in vandalism, masses of undergrowth and a lack of facilities, all of which frustrated the group. Undaunted, the first open day was held on 13 September 1975 to declare Llangollen station and a meagre 60 feet of track 'open', attracting some 1500 visitors!

Restoration and extension

The Llangollen Railway Society was set up in 1977, and the old Flint & Deeside Railway Preservation Society was wound up, transferring all its assets to the new society. Tracklaying commenced in earnest using

The early days of preservation: LMS 3F 'Jinty' tank No 7298 awaits departure from Llangollen towards Berwyn during the mid-1980s. *Peter Dickinson collection*

second-hand and donated track westwards from Llangollen station. Very few hand tools were available, let alone mechanical assistance, so laying the track had to be done the hard way. Sleepers were taken to the railhead on a small trolley and manhandled into position. Rails were laid in a similar fashion before alignment.

In July 1981 the Railway was inspected by the Railway Inspectorate and the first section of track was passed as fit for the use of passenger trains. Seven hundred passengers were carried on the first day and nearly 6,500 during the first operating season. Initially trains ran only to the site of the former Llangollen Goods Junction (then known as 'Ffordd Junction'), a distance of just over a quarter of a mile from Llangollen station.

The next major milestone was the extension of the line to the next station, Berwyn. The largest obstacle on this was the Dee Bridge, which required approximately £30,000 worth of work to be done on it. Fortunately, the local council came to the rescue with loans and grants enabling the work to be carried out in late 1984.

The first passenger train to Berwyn in 20 years ran in October 1985, when the Railway's diesel railcar ran as part of that year's Transport Extravaganza. Due to platform work being unfinished, passengers could not alight, but this was remedied in time for our first 'Santa Specials', which were run in December 1985. A full passenger service began in March 1986, with the formal opening ceremony being performed on 13 June by the Society's president, His Grace The Duke of Westminster.

1989 saw 'Project X' finally get off the ground, after thoughts of employing contractors were abandoned as unrealistically expensive. A team of volunteers banded together and got down to the serious business of rebuilding the railway to Deeside Halt. As the road access was at the Llangollen end of Berwyn Tunnel, tracklaying started from the far end and progressed back to join up with the existing railhead.

At Deeside Halt, a new two-coach platform was built, with an ex-GWR 'Pagoda' building being recovered by members from the old Festiniog station and rebuilt on it as a waiting room. Friday 2 March 1990 saw Major Olver of the Railway Inspectorate come to inspect the new extension, which was duly approved, apart from Deeside platform having to be lowered by 2 inches. This meant that passenger trains could begin once a few jobs had been completed. A special train, hauled by No 7828 *Odney Manor*, ran on Saturday 16 June, with a large number of guests. These included our President, His Grace the Duke of Westminster, who performed the opening ceremony, driving *Odney Manor* through a ceremonial white ribbon.

Burtonwood Brewer rests on shed at Llangollen in September 1990. This locomotive was built by Kitson & Co for the Austin Motor Company to work at the company's Longbridge plant, where it was known as *Austin 1*. Upon preservation in the 1970s, the locomotive was named *Burtonwood Brewer* in honour of the brewery, which paid for the restoration and fitting of vacuum brake gear required for working passenger trains. *Peter Dickinson collection*

There was hardly a pause for breath before 'Project X' restarted, perhaps better called 'Project Y', the next target being Glyndyfrdwy. The platforms there had been demolished on closure, and the site grassed over as a children's playing field. Excavation revealed the base of the original platforms, onto which the new platforms were built. In late 1990 a very dilapidated building was dismantled and recovered from Northwich, where it had been in use as the engine drivers' mess until it became derelict. This was re-erected on the new up platform in 1992 to serve as the station building, the original station building by now being in private hands.

Tracklaying began in March 1991, and moved on at high speed, with all the materials being available. Sleepers had been stockpiled at Glyndyfrdwy, from where they were loaded onto a lorry with a 'Hiab' and taken to the railhead. Rails were taken by rail from Llangollen to the railhead, where they were unloaded and towed by a tractor to the site.

By 24 May 1991 track was laid to within half a mile of Glyndyfrdwy village; 100 60-foot panels were laid in nine weeks. The first works train arrived on Sunday 21 July, although of course much work remained to be completed. A few weekends later the level crossing was laid. The first public passenger train to Glyndyfrdwy since 1964 arrived on 17 April 1992, headed by No 7822 *Foxcote Manor*. Subsequent work included the installation of the rest of the signalling and a footbridge, and the completion of Platform 2. The station and signal box received the Ian Allan National Railway Heritage Award in 1995.

Before the Carrog extension was even started, the station building there came up for sale, and was bought by a member of the Railway. A group called 'Friends of Carrog' was set up to organise the restoration of the station itself, and this got under way before the actual tracklaying began.

Work on the Carrog extension began in mid-July 1994 and progressed westwards over the following year. By late January 1996 the passing loop in Carrog station was virtually

Kitson & Co's No 5459 of 1932 was built for the Austin Motor Company to work at the Longbridge plant, where it was known as *Austin 1*. It is seen on display at Llangollen station shortly after its preservation and move to the line in 1975.

complete, with only 100 yards of track missing between the track laid in the station and the railhead of the single line back to Glyndyfrdwy. This gap was bridged on 4 February and the first passenger trains arrived on 2 May 1996.

Beyond Carrog, Corwen was the next town served by the Ruabon to Barmouth line, and in the new millennium became the target for the Llangollen Railway's next extension. In January 2012 volunteers began the task of laying track on the extension west of Carrog, and by early March the line extended 1,500 metres to Plas Bonwm Farm. This section was opened to the public during the steam mega-gala 'Steam, Steel & Stars 3' on 20 April 2012, with music mogul Pete Waterman cutting the tape; the first public train headed west hauled by the new-build steam locomotive No 60163 *Tornado* with No 7822 *Foxcote Manor* on the rear.

Tracklaying continued westwards, and on St David's Day 2015 the first passenger train arrived in Corwen. A temporary station platform had been constructed and carried the name 'Dwyrain Corwen East'. In its first ten days of operation, nearly 4,000 passengers sampled a ride on the extension from Carrog to Corwen.

Efforts then turned to constructing a brand-new terminus for the railway in Corwen, some 300 yards to the west of the temporary station. Corwen Central has been built at the site of a junction between the old Ruabon to Barmouth line and a branch northward towards Rhyl. Much work has been required to build a station from scratch here, including the installation of a subway, island platform, signal box and water tank. A gap in the trackbed (approximately 150 metres long and with a mean depth of 3 metres) required 1,000 tonnes of engineered fill to be brought in before the track could be laid. The temporary station at Dwyrain Corwen East closed to the public in November 2018, so that efforts could be focussed on completing Corwen Central.

Recreating the run-down and neglected state of Britain's steam railways in the 1960s, BR-built Manor No 7822 *Foxcote Manor* had been specially weathered for a 1960s gala weekend in 2011. *Peter Dickinson*

The Llangollen Railway adventure

The 10-mile journey along the Llangollen Railway from Llangollen to Corwen provides visitors with some extremely fine views of the Dee Valley that are denied to road visitors to the area. As you travel the length of the line, this guide aims to point out many of the things to look out for.

It is written starting from the Llangollen end of the line, but can be followed from the opposite direction too, although of course 'left' and 'right' will be reversed.

LLANGOLLEN

Standing prominently on the northern bank of the River Dee in the centre of town, Llangollen station is the main headquarters and eastern terminus of the Railway. The station dates back to 1865, replacing a temporary station from 1862 about a quarter of a mile

Looking towards the buffer stops, the station's footbridge offers a grandstand view as GWR pannier tank No 7714 begins to 'run around' its train in October 2018. *Kenny Felstead*

to the east. The arrival of the railway into the town required some major alterations to the historic Bishop Trevor Bridge, including the addition of an extra span at its northern end and the raising of the entire bridge deck to provide enough headroom to enable trains to pass through.

The main station building at Llangollen was built in a very distinctive style by the English architect Samuel Pountney Smith, who designed all the original station buildings on the Llangollen & Corwen Railway. His other works included St Collen's Church in the town, St Giles's Church in Shrewsbury, and the grand Llantysilio Hall near the Railway's station at Berwyn.

Ever since the station opened, Llangollen has been a popular destination for visitors and holidaymakers. The station was much enlarged around 1900 in order to cope with the lengthy excursion trains arriving from the Liverpool, Manchester and Birmingham areas. The sweeping S-shaped platforms and the canopied red-brick buildings that now house the Llangollen Railway's toilet facilities and offices all date from this time.

Before the departure of your train it is likely that the steam locomotive will have run around the loop, then been replenished with water from the tank on Llangollen's Platform 2, before running on and coupling up to the front of the train, ready for the off. At departure time the guard makes a final check with the station staff that no more passengers are expected, checks the doors are closed, blows his whistle and waves his green flag, giving the signal to the driver to open the locomotive's regulator to get the train moving.

Steam locomotives will often need to take water while at Llangollen station, so that they have enough in their tanks for the round trip to Corwen. Here we see GWR 'Large Prairie' No 5199 taking water at Llangollen during a gala event. During the 1950s and early 1960s local passenger trains were relatively short and consisted of only two or three coaches, as recreated here.
Clive Hanley

Fabulous floral displays can be seen at all our stations, particularly during the summer months. *Peter Dickinson*

Llangollen to Berwyn

As we depart from Llangollen station, the train passes under Green Lane bridge and begins to climb up the gradient through a short cutting and on to the river bank. The railway here originally featured double track to cope with the number of trains using the route from the east to Llangollen. Today the second track has been relaid as 'River Siding' and is used for stabling some of our historic railway carriages.

About half a mile out of the station, the Llangollen Goods Junction signal box is passed on the left. A spur from the locomotive shed drops down to meet us on the right at this point, while another spur heads off in the opposite direction towards the carriage and wagon workshops at Pentrefelin.

The locomotive workshops and shed for the LR's fleet of historic steam and diesel locomotives are located above the running line to the west of Llangollen station. In this view, GWR No 5643 is positioned in the shed yard over the maintenance pit, ready for examination between duties. *Matthew Collier*

The railway continues along the banks of the River Dee on the left; indeed, it is never more than half a mile away for the remainder of the journey to Corwen. Above the railway on the right, the Llangollen Canal can be glimpsed and will closely follow our route for the next mile. Traditional horse-drawn boats have been plying their trade along this stretch of the canal for more than 100 years and regularly operate out of Llangollen Wharf throughout the year.

As the line curves away to the left, the railway's carriage restoration workshops at Pentrefelin come into view. The site was originally developed to tranship slate from nearby quarries in the Berwyn Mountains onto railway wagons, and later developed into carriage sidings to house the stock from excursion trains arriving into Llangollen during the day. The large three-track workshop shed was completed in the late 1990s thanks to a Heritage Lottery Fund grant and is capable of housing up to nine carriages and three wagons. The site is also home to the railway's impressive fleet of heritage diesel multiple units (DMUs), which are owned and maintained by a dedicated group.

The line crosses over the river by the three-span Dee Bridge, which marks the start of the 1 in 80 climb for the next mile and a half through the Dee Gorge. The tumbling waters of the river below the line here are popular with canoeists, kayakers and white-water rafters.

BERWYN

Berwyn station (1½ miles from Llangollen) is prominently situated in the heart of the Dee Gorge and adjacent to Thomas Telford's main London to Holyhead road. The station was recently listed by the *Guardian* newspaper as being one of the Top 10 best railway stations to visit in Britain. The architect, Samuel Pountney Smith, headed his original drawings for the station in 1864 as a 'design for a second-class station', but as can be seen, this was anything but!

The substantial station building was built on a restricted site on a ledge overlooking the river. The mock-Tudor part of the building comprised the station master's house, which has now been restored as the Llangollen Railway's self-catered holiday cottage.

The central part of Berwyn station comprises the General Waiting Room, with an adjoining Booking Office. The elaborate lamps on the interior walls recall a time when the station was lit by oil and paraffin only, being too remote for gas pipes to be installed to it. The former 1st Class Waiting Room now hosts a small tearoom that is open most weekends during the operating season. Toilet facilities are available when the station is staffed.

Today Berwyn is located within an idyllic location with only a handful of houses and a riverside hotel nearby. However, in the Victorian era it was surrounded by several stately homes and a vibrant community including a local Post Office and Methodist chapel. Indeed, it was the landed gentry who were the main reason for the station's existence. The Chairman of the

Masquerading as a long-lost classmate, BR Standard No 80072 (running as No 80096) awaits departure from Berwyn in April 2014. *Peter Dickinson*

Autumnal colours at Berwyn. The former station master's house here is now the LR's holiday cottage. *Peter Dickinson*

Llangollen & Corwen Railway lived just up the road at Plas Berwyn mansion house and had an agreement to stop any passenger train at the station when he required.

The western part of the station platform is cantilevered along the side of the impressive six-arch Berwyn Viaduct, which straddles a stream and minor road. The platform was added in the early 1900s to cope with an increase in summer passenger numbers and was restored to its former glory in 2004.

The Station in the Gorge. *Peter Dickinson*

Berwyn to Glyndyfrdwy

Departing from Berwyn, the historic Chain Bridge crossing the river comes into view on the right. This is reputedly the oldest chain link bridge in the world. Its first incarnation was opened by a local entrepreneur called Exuperius Pickering in 1817 to transport his goods of coal, lime and iron bars across the river, avoiding the toll booths in Llangollen in the process!

After a short cutting, the Horseshoe Falls and the feeder stream to the Llangollen Canal are passed on the right. Around 12 million gallons of water are drawn in here each day from the River Dee to supply the canal system and provide south Cheshire with drinking water.

Immediately beyond, the impressive Llantysilio Hall was built in the 1870s for Charles Beyer, the celebrated railway locomotive designer and founder of Beyer, Peacock & Company in Manchester.

The line continues to climb for a further

The narrow nature of Berwyn Tunnel was often referred to by locomotive drivers as being like a 'cork in a bottle'. BR Standard No 80072 erupts from its eastern portal with a train heading towards Berwyn and Llangollen. *Clive Hanley*

A quintessential country branch line from the 1950s is recreated at Deeside Halt with a very special type of passenger train. This 'auto train' is formed of GWR Collett tank No 1450 sandwiched between two push-and-pull auto coaches, a precursor to modern diesel multiple units (DMUs). *Clive Hanley*

The daffodils are in full bloom as LMS Stanier Class 5 No 44806 rounds the curve at Garth-y-Dwr in April 2013. *Clive Hanley*

GWR 'Large Prairie' No 5199 passes Garth-y-Dwr on the approach to Glyndyfrdwy.
Kenny Felstead

half-mile to the 689-yard-long Berwyn Tunnel, the longest single-bore tunnel on any preserved railway in the UK. A lineside viewing area was installed at the eastern end of the tunnel in 2015 and has quickly become a popular photographic spot during gala events.

When the train re-emerges at the western end of Berwyn Tunnel, the line continues on a ledge high above the river. The reverse curves here offer a good view along the train to the steam locomotive working hard through the Dee Valley.

The valley begins to widen as the line swings around to the right and enters the passing loop at Deeside Halt. An unstaffed halt was opened here in the early 1990s and featured a simple wooden waiting shelter on a short ash-covered, timber-edged platform. The platform face was removed in early 2022 as a result of deterioration in the timbers. It is hoped that the Halt may be reinstated in the not too distant future.

After Deeside Halt, the line passes the wooded hillside of Pen y Garth before emerging alongside Garth-y-Dwr, a natural amphitheatre much loved by railway photographers. From here onwards the railway keeps the river on its right-hand side, and swings through an elongated S-bend towards the village of Glyndyfrdwy.

GLYNDYFRDWY

Glyndyfrdwy station (5½ miles from Llangollen) is an archetypal country station and the main passing loop on the railway. In GWR days it was at the centre of a booming trade in slate and slabs, which were quarried high up in the hills to the south. The extracted stone would then have been used to produce sills, doorsteps and slabs for flooring, as well as field and boundary posts.

The entrance into the station is marked by Glyndyfrdwy signal box on the right, which was recovered from Leaton near Shrewsbury. The line then crosses a minor road by means of a gated level crossing before entering the station platforms. The original station building is on the left but is now in private ownership. A traditional wooden station building is now in use on the right. Here there is a cosy tearoom and the Cambrian Bar, which are open during special events and galas throughout the year. Nearby a railway book and railwayana shop within a grounded carriage body raises vital funds for the 'Friends of Glyndyfrdwy Station'.

Glyndyfrdwy marks the middle of the journey between Llangollen and Corwen and is the main passing point for trains. GWR No 3802 enters into the station with a Llangollen-bound service, while BR Class 26 diesel No D5310 waits to proceed westwards. *Clive Hanley*

GWR pannier tank No 6430 is seen at Glyndyfrdwy operating in 'auto train' mode with a single auto coach. *Matthew Collier*

Visiting ex-LNWR 'Coal Tank' No 58926 awaits departure from Glyndyfrdwy, with Barmouth South signal box beyond. *Peter Dickinson*

Glyndyfrdwy to Carrog

Immediately after Glyndyfrdwy station the line passes the historic Barmouth South signal box, which was saved from destruction in the late 1980s and rebuilt brick by brick on its current site. It is hoped to convert the signal box into a dedicated signalling museum in due course. The line then hugs the riverbank as it gently curves around to the right; the proximity of the river makes this a particularly vulnerable section of track that receives constant inspection. A small footpath crossing over the railway here gives local fishermen access to the river and also links to the 'Berwyn Arms' public house, which is immediately above us to our left.

From here the Dee Valley broadens out and there are good views of both the Berwyn and Llantysilio Mountains, dotted with hill farms and cottages. This stretch of line was used as the location for the railway sequences in the 2014 film *Mr Turner*.

About a mile east, the line enters into a wooded cutting on the edge of the River Dee. This is the foot of 'Owain Glyndwr's Mount', which was reputedly the site of Owain Glyndwr's manor house. It was from here in September 1400 that he proclaimed himself Prince of Wales, so beginning his 14-year rebellion against English rule. The mount itself is actually the remains of a 12th-century castle motte, built to command the main route through the Dee Valley.

Carrog station is then approached as the train follows a long reverse curve across the wide river meadows, giving good views of the station from the left of the train.

The section of line westwards from Glyndyfrdwy was used as the location for the railway sequences in the 2014 film *Mr Turner*. GWR tank locomotive No 5643 scurries over Fisherman's Crossing with a Llangollen to Carrog service. *Clive Hanley*

CARROG

The precursor of the 'auto train' was the GWR steam railmotor. The now unique 1908-built Railmotor No 93 and accompanying 1912-built trailer No 92 depart from Carrog during a rare visit away from their home at Didcot Railway Centre in 2013. *Matthew Collier*

Carrog Station (7½ miles from Llangollen) has been meticulously rebuilt by volunteers to how it was in the 1950s. Here can be found a place where time has stood still.

The station is located on a gentle left-hand curve, with a signal box, two sidings and a restored cattle dock on the right. The slate station building, comprising the ticket office, waiting room and tearoom, stands on the right-hand platform alongside a dedicated toilet building. A brick-built waiting shelter is located opposite this on the left-hand platform, housing a small museum dedicated to the history of the line.

Although very little appears to have changed at Carrog since GWR and BR days, many of the buildings and infrastructure have had to be rebuilt. Only seven or eight incomplete courses of brick remained of the station's signal box when restoration began, and this has been painstakingly rebuilt to an operational condition.

A redundant GWR waiting room building from Weston-sub-Edge on the northern half of the Cheltenham-Stratford line was bought for a mere £200 in 1994. Thirty volunteers took three days to carefully demolish the building and palletise the bricks for reconstruction on Platform 2 at Carrog.

The historic infrastructure today provides

BR Standard No 80072 heads a demonstration freight train in Carrog station. A dedicated sales coach within the station yard assists with the ongoing maintenance and overhaul costs of this historic steam locomotive. *Clive Hanley*

the opportunity to display such early period features as signs, advertisements, posters, milk churns, cabin trunks and, of course, elaborate floral displays in the station gardens in season.

Railwayana and book shops within a pair of former railway carriages alongside the station's cattle dock raise vital funds towards some of the steam locomotives based on the line.

A visiting BR Class 25 diesel (affectionately known as 'Rats') hauls a demonstration engineering train into Carrog in 2019. *Matthew Collier*

Carrog to Corwen

The waiting room on the Down platform at Carrog now oozes ambience and atmosphere following restoration by the line's Heritage Group.
Peter Dickinson'

On departure from Carrog the train passes under a minor lane and through a minor cutting before rejoining the banks of the River Dee. A short blast on the whistle marks the crossing of a popular public footpath linking the A5 road with Carrog's historic village. In such a rural idyll, it is worth remembering that our passenger trains only started using this section of the line as recently as 2012!

At the point where the river and railway

With the first signs of autumn appearing in the Dee Valley, Great Western Railway 0-6-0 pannier tank No 7714 approaches the foot crossing just to the west of Carrog station in October 2018.
Kenny Felstead

Prior to the opening of Corwen Central, passenger services westwards from Carrog were often 'top-and-tailed' during special events. In March 2017 LMS 'Flying Pig' No 43106 approaches Corwen with a BR Standard tank locomotive attached to the rear of the train. *Kenny Felstead*

diverge again, there was originally a short siding on the left serving a small slate wharf. From here a narrow-gauge tramway climbed up to Penarth Quarry, above and south of the A5 road. The tramway closed during the 1930s.

Immediately beyond, Plas Bonwm Farm on the left of the train marks the position of the former stop block for passenger trains between 2012 and 2014. The lineside here was used for stockpiling the tonnes of stone ballast needed during the railway's reinstatement.

Beyond the farm, the line appears sandwiched between the A5 road and the River Dee on its approach to Corwen. In 1935 a small wayside halt was opened at Bonwm, the location now being where the A5 swings in to run parallel with the line. The halt was a very basic affair, being only long enough to accommodate one passenger carriage, and boasted a simple wooden shelter, station nameboard and an electric light. There are currently no plans to reinstate this halt in the near future.

The line beyond Bonwm is almost perfectly straight until it reaches the outskirts of Corwen. A traditional wooden hut has been carefully restored on the right; it would have been used as a refuge for the local track workers up until the 1960s. After passing through a fine stone overbridge, the line gently swings round to the right before entering our western terminus of Corwen.

CORWEN

Our first passenger trains returned to Corwen in 2015, but initially this was to a temporary station at Dwyrain Corwen East. This was a fairly modest affair; comprising a single platform built of scaffolding and lacking any sort of run-round loop. Trains departing back towards Llangollen either had to have a locomotive at each end, or be propelled for 2½ miles using a second driver within a specially adapted brake carriage. This arrangement came to an end in November 2018, after which time the temporary platform was dismantled and most trains terminated at Carrog.

The Llangollen Railway has built a brand-new station offering a grandstand position overlooking the centre of the town. It is ideally placed adjacent to Corwen's bus station and large car park. In contrast to the Llangollen Railway's four original stations, the design of Corwen's new station boasts an island platform arrangement, which can accommodate an eight-coach train on one side and a five-coach

One of the largest locomotives to be built by British Railways was the Standard 9F heavy freight engine. Visiting 9F No 92214 *Central Star* approaches Corwen during 2015. *Clive Hanley*

train on the other. Access is gained through a subway under the tracks and up a flight of stairs. To assist our less mobile visitors, a stairlift has been carefully included into the design and installed during construction.

The former Weston Rhyn signal box from the Chester to Shrewsbury line has been rebuilt and restored at the eastern end of the station. In time this signal box will control all the train movements in and around the station. However, the section from Carrog to Corwen is initially being operated using a 'one train

working' system and the trackwork controlled using simple ground-mounted lever frames.

A large water tank has also been installed at the eastern end of the station. This allows our steam locomotive the opportunity to have its tanks replenished with water, in readiness for the return working eastwards towards Llangollen. The water is not pumped directly from the river, but rather from a dedicated 50-metre-deep borehole that has been drilled adjacent to the station.

The station throat into Corwen Central being constructed during 2020. The rebuilt Weston Rhyn signal box will control all train movements around the station once commissioned.
George Jones

The steam locomotive fleet – a selection

Most Llangollen Railway services are hauled by steam locomotives. The line plays host to a fleet of regular and visiting locomotives, the youngest of which are now around 70 years old. These next few pages feature a selection of steam locomotive that have been seen on the Llangollen Railway's metals in recent years.

After ten years' operation all steam locomotives require a complete strip-down for a boiler overhaul and insurance inspection. The opportunity is taken at this time to examine and repair all the other parts of the engine. These overhauls can take many months or even years and require both large sums of money and specialist workshop skills.

No 3802 is a GWR Collett '2884' Class 2-8-0 locomotive and is a regular performer on the Llangollen Railway. Eighty-three members of the class were built by the Great Western Railway between 1938 and 1941. They were a Collett development of the successful Churchward 2800 Class, developed early in the 20th century. The class was designed to handle long distance heavy freight trains, so their average job would have been to haul large rakes of wagons at speed around 20-30 mph over distances of 100-200 miles. *Peter Dickinson*

Top right: BR Standard tank No 80072 is one of the youngest locomotives in the LR's current fleet, with construction having been completed at Brighton in 1953! *Matthew Collier*

Centre right: Upon its withdrawal by BR in 1964, pannier tank No 6430 was originally preserved only as a source of spares to keep two fellow classmates steaming. Fortunately, it was bought as a kit of parts by its present owner in 1990 and after an extensive restoration it moved under its own steam in December 2003. *Clive Hanley*

Bottom right: GWR 'Large Prairie' No 5199 pilots a BR 'Manor' Class locomotive during the climb through the woods near Berwyn Tunnel. No 5199 was originally built in 1934 and spent most of its working life hauling suburban passenger services around Birmingham. After withdrawal in 1963 and languishing for 22 years in a scrapyard in South Wales, restoration commenced and the locomotive steamed again in early 2003. *Clive Hanley*

Some iconic main-line steam locomotives have visited the Llangollen Railway, usually as 'stars' of steam gala events. Here are three of them.

Right: British Railways 4-6-2 No 70000 *Britannia was* the first of 55 express passenger locomotives built by British Railways, emerging from Crewe in January 1951.
Peter Dickinson

London Midland & Scottish Railway 5MT 2-6-0 No 42968 pauses at Glyndyfrdwy in April 2010.
Matthew Collier

Great Western Railway 2-6-0 No 5322 approaches Berwyn during the 2014 Spring Steam Gala.
Peter Dickinson

Feeding the line. *Richard Smith*

The diesel fleet – a selection

Loco No	Class	Wheel arr.	Builder	Year built	Weight (tons)
Ex-British Railways					
D1566 (47449)	47	Co-Co	Crewe	1964	127 0
(D2162) 03162	03	0-6-0	Swindon	1960	30 16
(D3265, 08195) 13265	08	0-6-0	Derby	1956	49 0
D5310 (26010)	26	Bo-Bo	Smethwick	1958	77 0
Ex-industrial					
1901 *Davy*	-	0-6-0	ICI	1951	
2892 *Pilkington*	-	0-4-0	Yorkshire Engineering	-	
2899	-	0-4-0	Yorkshire Engineering	-	

BR Class 26 diesel No D5310 rounds the bend eastwards out of Glyndyfrdwy with a passenger service to Llangollen. *Peter Dickinson*

D1566 *Orion* (later numbered 47449) is a Crewe-built, series-parallel wired Brush Type 4 (Class 47) – the only remaining Brush Type 4 of this less common pedigree. The loco has been a member of the fleet at Llangollen since 1996. *Richard Smith*

The mainstay of shunting work on the Llangollen Railway is BR/English Electric 350hp 0-6-0 diesel shunting locomotive No 13265 (Class 08 No 08195). *Peter Dickinson*

Delivered new from BR Swindon works to York on 21 September 1960, Class 03 shunter No 03162 has proved invaluable on construction trains for the Corwen extension. *Peter Dickinson*

The Llangollen railcar fleet

DMU Vehicle No	Class	Builder	Type	Year built
50416	109	Wickham of Ware	Driving Motor Brake	1957
50447	104	Birmingham RC&W Co	Driving Motor Brake	1957
50454	104	Birmingham RC&W Co	Driving Motor Brake	1957
50528	104	Birmingham RC&W Co	Driving Motor Composite	1957
51118	100	Gloucester RC&W Co	Driving Motor Brake	1957
51618	127	BR Derby	Driving Motor Brake	1959
51907	108	BR Derby	Driving Motor Brake	1960
51933	108	BR Derby	Driving Motor Brake	
54504	108	BR Derby	Driving Trailer Composite	
54490	108	BR Derby	Driving Trailer Composite	1960
55513	141	BR Derby and Leyland Buses, Workington	-	1984
55533	141	BR Derby and Leyland Buses, Workington	-	1984
56097	100	Gloucester RC&W Co	Driving Trailer Composite	1957
56171	109	Wickham of Ware	Driving Trailer Composite	1957
56223	108	BR Derby	Driving Trailer Composite	1959
56456	105	Cravens, Sheffield	Driving Trailer Composite	1958

LLANGOLLEN RAILWAY

A BR blue-and-grey-liveried Class 108 DMU, passing over the Dee Bridge, is greeted by friendly waves from the rafters on the river below. *Peter Dickinson*

The line's unique Class 109 'Wickham' DMU awaits departure from Llangollen with a Carrog-bound service. *Peter Dickinson*

A BR Class 104 DMU pauses at Berwyn during a winter's evening. *Clive Hanley*

Passenger coaches

British Railways, 1948-1997: Formed from the nationalisation of the 'Big Four' railway companies, the LNER, LMS, GWR and SR. The Llangollen Railway has examples from the 1950s and early 1960s, including some of the suburban carriages that would have been regularly used by commuters in and out of London's King's Cross station. The majority of our British Railways coaches are open plan with bays of four seats arranged around tables, but there are a small number with side corridors and compartments. This is Tourist 2nd Open No 4472 of 1957. *Kenny Felstead*

Hawksworth-designed engineers' saloon No 80975 built at Swindon in 1948 and is well-suited for private hire, offering a panoramic view of the line. *Peter Dickinson*

Goods vehicles

The Railway operates a demonstration freight train at most steam galas and other special occasions. This is the eastern approach to Berwyn Tunnel in March 2017. The wagons have been bought and restored by volunteers in the workshops at Pentrefelin. The result, as seen here, is a very credible BR goods train headed appropriately by Stanier Class 5 No 45337, which had been renumbered as a long-lost classmate for the occasion and suitably weathered using poster paint! *Kenny Felstead*

Another outing for the demonstration freight train came in April 2018, and it is seen approaching Glyndyfrdwy, with GWR pannier No 6430 providing the power. *Peter Dickinson*

WWI soldiers' poignant messages at Berwyn

From its opening until at least the mid-1890s, Berwyn station was connected by an access path to the Chain Bridge over the River Dee. This path crossed over the railway line at the eastern end of the platform and this became the scene for a fatal accident just a few days before Christmas in 1896. On Tuesday 22 December Charles Roberts, a Blacksmith and his wife Jane had been visiting friends near the station. Shortly after 9pm they were on their way home and as they approached the ungated crossing heard a train approaching them. Assuming this was the mail train that was due to stop at Berwyn they continued across the track. Unfortunately it was a 'special' put on to cope with the increased amounts of mail being carried in the run up to the festive period. The crank of the steam locomotive caught the side of Jane Roberts's head and her body was found about fifteen yards from the crossing.

Charles Roberts sued the Great Western Railway and received substantial damages. The fatality and the increasing popularity of the walking route led to the Great Western Railway deciding to remove the crossing completely and replace it with a pedestrian underpass. A steep pathway was excavated adjacent to the railway, almost as a continuation of the platform ramp, leading to a short 6-foot wide tunnel under the one railway track. The structure in itself may have been fairly unremarkable, but for the fact that it was finished in white glazed bricks. The bricks seemed to have taken pencil markings readily, especially from the indelible type issued to soldiers during the First World War. Teenage conscripts used their pencils to write notes on the subway's walls and many of these still survive today, albeit becoming increasingly at risk from water ingress and deterioration.

One entry on the walls shows that E. M. Morris and R. Roberts shared a cigarette together there on 6 July 1913. By the time they returned on Christmas Day the following year, they had both enlisted in the Army and had quickly been promoted. Indeed R. Roberts signed his festive message with the ranking of a Lance Corporal. Some of the other scribblings indicated soldiers in light-hearted mood, including 'Balls from Belgium', 'Berlin Last Stop' and 'Hoof Hearted'. Over subsequent years, the walls of the subway continued to attract more notes and messages in pencil up until at least the 1960s when the railway closed. In our modern society, graffiti is often seen as defacement and vandalism in most situations. Yet after the passage of a century, the written WWI messages on the subway walls have become poignant and important historical artefacts in their own right.

Eat & drink at the Llangollen Railway

A traditional cream tea with a slice of nostalgia on offer at Berwyn station.

Off-train catering

Llangollen: The Station Café & Bar opens well before the first train of the day, allowing plenty of time to enjoy a freshly cooked breakfast prior to travelling on the train. Throughout the day a wide variety of freshly prepared sandwiches, hot food specials, soups, confectionery and desserts are available.

Berwyn: The station's **Tearoom** offers a range of hot and cold drinks, snacks and homemade cakes at weekends and busy times.

Glyndyfrdwy: The station's **Tearoom** and licensed **Cambrian Bar** are open only during special events and are a great place to meet for a glass or two from a selection of real ales during gala weekends.

Carrog: The station's **Tearoom** is open on all operating days offering tea, coffee, freshly made sandwiches, pasties and homemade cakes.

Dine on the line

Looking for that extra-special treat? Imagine sitting back, relaxing in the stunning Welsh countryside and enjoying a freshly prepared tea as you steam through the Dee Valley. On-board dining options include Welsh Cream Teas, Picnics, Buffet Lunches and Afternoon Teas.

Our Afternoon Teas include a selection of finger sandwiches, cream tea and a selection of treats/cakes with optional upgrades with alcoholic drinks including wines, Prosecco and Champagne.

Galas and special events
Example Events

- Autumn Steam Gala
- Classic Transport Weekend
- Heritage Railcar Gala
- Autumn Diesel Gala
- Sensational 60s & 70s Themed Weekend
- 1940s Weekend
- Day out with Thomas™
- Mothers Day and Fathers Day Specials
- Real Ale Trains
- Fish and Chip Special
- Gin Train
- Murder Mystery Specials
- Oktoberfest
- Halloween Train
- Ride the Rocket Firework Train
- Santa Specials and Mince Pie Specials

Ask for full details, including dates and times, at our Booking Offices.

Steam gala events are often held over extended weekends during the year and feature visiting steam locomotives operating alongside the line's home fleet. In this scene at Carrog station from 2015, SR Bulleid 'Pacific' locomotive No 34092 *Wells* stands alongside fellow visitor BR Standard 9F No 92214 *Central Star*. *Clive Hanley*

Making a very rare venture south from its native Scotland, Caledonian Railway No 828 looks very much at home as it passes Garth-y-Dwr during a 'Steel, Steam & Stars' mega-gala in 2012. *Clive Hanley*

A gathering of vintage Willys Jeeps on the station ramp at Llangollen in May 2019. These charismatic vehicles were designed by the US Army to 'go anywhere and do anything' during the Second World War. Vintage cars, motorbikes, buses and commercial road vehicles form the centrepiece of the LR's Classic Transport Weekend, which is usually held in early July. *Peter Dickinson*

The LR's 1940s Weekend is an event usually held in mid-September. All the line's stations take part, with re-enactors performing, memorabilia displays and live musical performances. Here a group of 1940s re-enactors promise that they 'will meet again' on Llangollen station platform. *Peter Dickinson*

The Llangollen Railway – more than just a train ride!

Driver Experience courses

Accompanied and guided by an experienced Llangollen Railway driver, take the driving seat on one of our full-sized steam or diesel locomotives as you wind your way along the Dee Valley.

Our Steam Locomotive, Diesel Locomotive and Heritage Railcar (DMU) Experiences enable the participant to drive on the 15-mile round trip from Llangollen to Carrog. 'Evening Ramble' opportunities are available, offering the participant the chance to drive and fire a light steam engine (without carriages) from Llangollen to Carrog and back.

Our 'All Day Freight Experience' gives the participant the chance to drive, fire, assist the guard and try their hand at shunting. These experiences are ideal for individuals or for groups of up to six people.

Looking for a unique gift present? Open gift vouchers are available that are valid for 13 months from the date of purchase.

Railway weddings

The Railway's Henry Robertson suite at Llangollen Station is licensed for weddings and civil ceremonies. We specialise in providing a personal and unique venue for those who are looking for a small intimate ceremony with a truly relaxing experience for you and your guests. The venue can seat a maximum of 64 people (including the happy couple of course!) and will be prepared with floral displays. Afterwards, you can hire your very own steam-hauled carriage for a trip along the line as you and your guests enjoy your wedding breakfast. We also can arrange your evening celebrations and you can even hire your own private train.

With many different catering options for food and drink, as well as quirky photo opportunities, the Llangollen Railway will leave lasting impressions for years to come.

GWR pannier tank No 6430 makes an impressive sight passing Garth-y-Dwr with a Corwen to Llangollen service. *Clive Hanley*

Supporting the Railway

The Llangollen Railway's purpose is to 'preserve, maintain and operate the LR as a working museum and tourist attraction for the education and enjoyment of present and future generations'. Since its inception in the early 1970s, a 10-mile section of railway has been painstakingly rebuilt so that trains can once again link the towns of Llangollen and Corwen. It now carries some 100,000 passengers each year. Operated by around 200 working volunteers who give up their time to restore and run our heritage trains and maintain the historic infrastructure, it is supported by approximately 40 employees.

'Llangollen Railway' is an umbrella name for the following organisation.

Llangollen Railway Trust Limited is a company limited by guarantee and exists to raise funds to further the development of the railway. Trust membership helps the railway financially, while also offering the benefits of concessionary travel and complimentary copies of the Trust's *Steam at Llangollen* magazine. Membership of the Trust also provides insurance cover for those who wish to volunteer on the Railway.

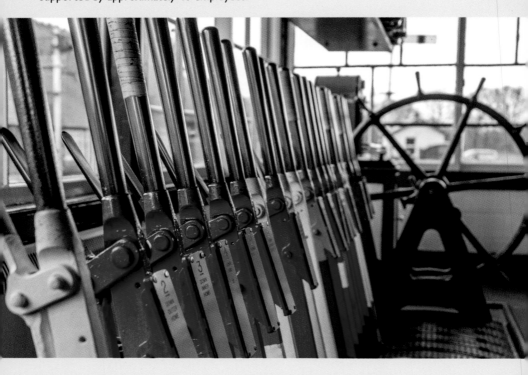

Signal boxes are crucial to the safe operation of trains on the Llangollen Railway. These traditional levers within Glyndyfrdwy signal box control all the points and signals around the station. Operating the levers often requires a lot of strength on the part of the signalman, particularly for the signals furthest away from the station! *Clive Hanley*

Would you like to help us?

The majority of the people you will meet running the Railway will be enjoying their spare time as much as you are. Volunteers undertake all the jobs that are essential for the safe and smooth operation of the Railway, both the jobs that might first come to mind, as well as many that may go unnoticed but are nonetheless essential to making the trains run, whether that is:

- Selling tickets
- Helping passengers onto our trains
- Keeping our stations and coaches clean and tidy
- Being part of our on-train crews – as guard, fireman, engine cleaner, ticket inspector or even as driver
- Caring for and restoring our heritage rolling stock
- Working on keeping our fleets of steam locomotives, diesel locomotives and heritage railcars running

- Safely signalling our trains up and down the line
- Restoring and maintaining our stations and gardens
- Keeping our track in good order
- Maintaining drains, bridges and structures, many of which are more than 150 years old
- Managing the vegetation and environmental ecosystems along our scenic line

To find out more about membership and volunteering, please visit www.llangollen-railway.co.uk, or pick up a leaflet at one of our manned stations during your visit.

The Llangollen Railway can accept volunteers who are under the age of 18. Our Youth Group encourages boys and girls from the age of 12 to take an active part in the operation of the railway by allowing them to work alongside adult volunteers.

Volunteers hard at work restoring one of the line's historic foot crossings near Carrog.

Spotting along the way

From Llangollen to Corwen:

1. **Spot suitcases on both platforms.** Score 5 points if you see them. How many can you count?
2. **Spot the signalman by his signal box.** Score 5 points or 10 points if he is carrying the hooped train token.
3. **Spot camping coaches high up above the railway.** Score 5 points. Our locomotive crews and volunteers often stay in these.
4. **Spot Clarabel in the carriage sidings.** Score 5 points. Can you see Thomas' other friends too?
5. **Spot the River Dee on BOTH sides of the train.** Score 5 points. You're now crossing the Dee Bridge.
6. **Spot a chain bridge over the river at Berwyn.** Score 5 points. This is possibly the oldest chain link bridge in the World.
7. **Spot a 'Brooke Bond Tea' sign at Berwyn station.** Score 5 points.
8. **Spot the Horseshoe Falls below the railway.** Score 5 points. This was built by Thomas Telford in 1808 to guide water into the start of the Llangollen canal, 13 million gallons of water flow over here per day.
9. **Spot a long tunnel.** Score 5 points. You would need to be asleep to miss this one!
10. **Spot Deeside Halt whizzing past the window.** Score 10 points. Trains will only stop here on request or to pass other trains on the line.
11. **Spot the level crossing at Glyndyfrdwy.** Score 5 points. How many cars are waiting behind the gates for our train to pass? Spot fishermen fishing from the riverbank. Keep a sharp lookout and score 10 points. Spot silver milk churns on the platform at CaRrog. Score 5 points.
12. **Spot red fire buckets hanging from the station building.** Score 5 points. Hopefully they will never be needed! Spot Carrog village on the opposite riverbank. Score 5 points. The village was originally called Glyndyfrdwy Llansantffraid - imagine the confusion if it was still called this today! Spot the farmyard and barn beside the line. Score 5 points.
13. **Spot a tall yellow signal.** Score 5 points. This tells the driver to slow down because the next signal may be at the horizontal 'stop' position.
14. **Spot the large grey water tower on the platform at Corwen.** Score 5 points and 10 more if you see a steam locomotive being filled up from it.

95 – 120   *Excellent! Top Spotter!*
65 – 90   *You're good at spotting along the Dee Valley!*
35 – 60   *Keep a look out next time you travel with us!*
0 – 30   *There's plenty to see and do along the beautiful Dee Valley! Keep spotting!*

Lineside signs

The location of stations, bridges and other structures on the railway are measured from a datum point (normally a major terminus such as London Paddington). On the Llangollen Railway, the datum point used is where the line used to join with the rest of the national network – around ¾ mile south of Ruabon station at the former Llangollen Line Junction. The Railways Clauses Consolidation Act 1845 Section 94 stated 'The company shall cause the length of the railway

A newly restored milepost near Plas Bonwm Farm.

to be measured, and milestones, posts, or other conspicuous objects to be set up and maintained along the whole line thereof, at the distance of one quarter of a mile from each other, with numbers or marks inscribed thereon denoting such distances'. Mileposts showing the distance from the long-lost Llangollen Line Junction can still be seen today and are visible along the north side of the line. The first one you will likely encounter is Milepost 5½, located on the platform at Llangollen station. The series of vertical 'strokes' beneath the mileage denotes the relevant number of quarter miles. The railway's Heritage Group are currently restoring and reinstating many of the original mileposts along the line – the majority of these examples being around Glyndyfrdwy and Carrog stations. Keep an eye out for these from your carriage window as the train steams alongside the picturesque River Dee. The other prominent posts along the lineside are the gradient posts. These are located at places where there are significant changes in the gradient of the track. Semaphore arms that indicate and express the applicable gradients are attached to opposite sides of the main vertical post. The steepest gradient is the 1-in-80 climb faced by trains leaving Llangollen up Berwyn Bank.

A gradient post on the south side of the line at Glyndyfrdwy station.

Spotlight on Garth-y-Dwr

Recreating the summer holiday trains that once carried excited holidaymakers to the Cambrian Coast, two BR-built 'Manor' locomotives pass Garth-y-Dwr in April 2016. *Dave Bowles*

An evening glint catches ex-LNWR 'Super D' 0-8-0 No 49395 passing Garth-y-Dwr with a photographic charter in 2012. *Dave Bowles*